WOODWORKING PROJECTS

for the Garden

WOODWORKING
PROJECTS
for the Garden

40 Fun & Useful Things for Folks Who Garden

Richard Freudenberger

A Sterling/Lark Book
Sterling Publishing Co., Inc.   New York

Editor: Chris Rich
Art Director: Kathleen Holmes
Production: Elaine Thompson and Kathleen Holmes
Illustrations: Don Osby
Photography: Evan Bracken

Library of Congress Cataloging-in-Publication Data
Freudenberger, Richard
    Woodworking projects for the garden : 40 fun & useful things for folks
who garden / Richard Freudenberger.
      p.   cm.
    "A Sterling/ Lark book."
    Includes index.
    1. Woodwork--Amateurs' manuals.   2. Garden ornaments and furniture--
Design and construction--Amateurs' manuals.
   3. Gardening--Equipment and supplies--Design and construction--
Amateurs' manuals.   I. Title.
TT185.F74   1994
684. 1'8--dc20   94-7981
                                                         CIP

10 9 8 7 6 5 4 3 2 1

A Sterling/Lark Book

Published in 1994 by Sterling Publishing Company, Inc.
  387 Park Avenue South, New York, N.Y. 10016

Produced by Altamont Press, Inc.
  50 College Street, Asheville, NC 28801

© 1994 by Altamont Press

Distributed in Canada by Sterling Publishing,
  c/o Canadian Manda Group, P.O. Box 920, Station U,
  Toronto, Ontario, Canada M8Z 5P9
Distributed in Great Britain and Europe by Cassell PLC, Villiers House,
  41/47 Strand, London WC2N 5JE, England
Distributed in Australia by Capricorn Link (Australia) Pty Ltd.
  P.O. Box 6651, Baulkham Hills, Business Centre, NSW 2153, Australia

Every effort has been made to ensure that all information in this book is accurate. However, due to differing conditions, tools, and individual skills, the publisher cannot be responsible for any injuries, losses, or other damages which may result from the use of the information in this book.

The projects in this book are the original creations of the contributing designers. They may be reproduced by individuals for personal pleasure; reproduction on a larger scale with the intent of personal profit is prohibited.

Printed in Hong Kong by Regent Publishing

Sterling ISBN 0-8069-0802-5

❧ CONTENTS ❧

INTRODUCTION

What do avid woodworkers and gardeners share? The desire to work with Mother Nature instead of against her. The patience and flexibility to adapt to her demands. A certain degree of organization, of course, and the healthy suspicion that life offers few activities as satisfying as working with the materials that nature provides.

If you're tempted to let your lack of woodworking or gardening experience hold you back from enjoying this book, think about the qualities that we've just described. You won't need much more in order to build the projects presented within these pages. With a few basic woodworking tools, a steady hand, and a willingness to learn, almost any of these forty attractive, useful garden accessories is well within your reach. And so what if you don't have backyard space in which to use them? They make terrific gifts for folks who do.

Beginning woodworkers will find all the help they'll need: hints on how to select a project and plan a workshop, descriptions of every required tool and material, a comprehensive chapter on woodworking techniques, step-by-step construction procedures, and detailed, exploded-view illustrations. Woodworkers with more experience will find ample challenges, too; the Gazebo and Footbridge projects should test their mettle.

Whether you're new to working with wood or an expert already, a gardener or a friend to one, you'll soon discover that our projects have been designed with real woodworkers and real gardeners in mind; they're all sturdy and useful. What's more, while they'll certainly help to transform old gardening frustrations into new gardening pleasures, they're also handsome. The Flower Truck, for example, will do its job as well as or better than any commercial counterpart, but it's so attractive that you may end up deciding to use it as a vase.

The one drawback to making these projects is that the act of woodworking itself can become addictive—just as addictive as using what you make to improve your garden. The scent of fresh wood shavings or of rich loam in spring, the unforgettable feel of a well-sanded bench top or table, the startling taste of tomatoes warm off the vine—there's nothing quite like the satisfaction of shaping and tending nature's bounties. In today's high-tech, high-speed world, however, why bother to kick these habits? They're relaxing, productive, and downright fun.

GROUNDWORK

A child's first garden is likely to be harvested about four to eight weeks too early. Why? Think back a few years. When you were seven or eight years old, did patience stand a chance against the excitement of seeing and touching your very own, live vegetables? Nope. And what was the result? Family salads that harbored a lot of miniature carrots and marble-sized radishes.

There's not a thing wrong with the wild enthusiasm that beginning gardeners often feel. In fact, many of us could probably use a hefty dose in our adult lives. But as gardeners get older, they learn that reaping carrots large enough to chew and taste takes planning, preparation, and patience, too.

Beginning woodworkers face a similar situation. There's nothing quite like that first whiff of cedar or the pleasant hum of a fine power saw, but first-time builders who rush through their projects often end up with items that they don't really need and won't often use.

Setting up a workshop, getting to know your tools, and taking safety precautions as you work are all-important steps, ones that will ensure a successful and enjoyable woodworking venture. The better organized you are before you start, the less time you'll waste searching for what you need and correcting your mistakes as you build. You'll also waste less wood. As our forests dwindle and the cost of lumber climbs, saving wood in the workshop becomes more and more important.

THE WORKSHOP

For readers who are starting out from scratch, the place to begin is in the workshop, where tools, project materials, hardware, and supplies are stored and used. Workshops are as different as their owners, but good ones bear several characteristics in common; they're dry, well ventilated, well lit, adequately wired for electricity, and well organized.

• If your space isn't dry, your tools and hardware may rust.

• Good ventilation is a must; floating sawdust and toxic fumes will do more damage to your body than any amount of unwelcome water will do to your projects and tools. Install a ventilating fan if possible, or keep a room fan in one window to pull tainted air away from you.

• Lights should be bright enough to allow you to measure and mark accurately and to keep an eye on moving blades and bits.

• Electrical service should be sufficient for your tools and properly fused, and all outlets should be grounded.

Keeping your workshop organized is a habit like any other, though not always, we'll admit, an easy one to learn. Unless you're already one of those people who remembers to replace the cap on your toothpaste tube, you may have to work to develop this time-saving (and life-protecting) woodworking behavior. Here's how to begin.

Whether you're designing your work area as you read these pages or evaluating space that you already have, think in terms of designating a permanent home for every object in it. Juggle its contents mentally or sketch a few workshop plans until you're comfortable with the location of every item. Then, whenever you're finished with a given woodworking task, send whatever was in your hands back home.

Keep hand-held tools on pegboards. Mark their locations on the board by tracing the tools' shapes with a marker. These outlines will remind you where each tool belongs. Hot-glue those pegboard hooks in place to keep them from dropping out every time you grab for a tool. Label shelves and drawers, too. Eventually, you'll no longer need these clean-up cues, but in the meantime they'll save a lot of time.

SELECTING A PROJECT

We're sure that you'll like at least one of the projects in this book, but you may have trouble deciding which one to build first. Following are some hints to help you narrow down your choices.

• First, pick several projects that appeal to your visual taste. Building something just because you think you need it is not the way to go! If a functional project makes you shudder every time you see it, it's likely to languish untouched.

• Then, think about which of these choices you and your family would most enjoy. The Portable Shade Screen's design might strike you as simply stunning, but if your entire backyard is already shaded by the neighborhood's largest oak tree, build the screen for a friend, and select another project for yourself.

• Next, decide where to put the project. Take a good look at the illustrations that accompany it, and compare their dimensions with the dimensions of the garden site that you've chosen. Imagined space is almost always larger than real space, especially after you've caught the woodworking bug. You'll save a lot of lumber by matching your desire with reality!

• For projects that will live outdoors, look closely at the site you've chosen, and imagine your completed project in it. Does the wood that we recommend clash in any way with its surroundings—the siding on your home or the deck or patio material? If so, choose another wood species or paint the project to complement its future environment. Make sure that the project won't make your outdoor spot look awkward or cluttered, though; short of changing the landscape, there's little you can do to improve on the way that it fits in.

• Consider expenses. We can't provide cost estimates for you, but we can tell you how to come up with some figures yourself. First, look at the lists of materials and supplies; these come with every project. Then call—or better yet, browse through—your local lumberyard (or specialty wood supplier) and hardware store to get current prices. If you intend to make more than a single project, buying in bulk may save you money. Renting or borrowing tools can be economical, too. And remember that our wood recommendations aren't written in stone; if you need to substitute a less expensive wood, go right ahead.

• Think about how much time you have. The stunning Gazebo project might be perfect for your outdoor property, but if handling a job, cooking the meals, tending the kids, and walking the dog leave you without much extra energy, line up some helping hands before you tackle this one. It's likely to take even an accomplished woodworker several weekends to make.

• Your woodworking skill level should probably be the least of your concerns. With the exception of the

Footbridge and Gazebo, most of our projects are well within reach of beginners. Some of the construction techniques, however, do depend on your being comfortable using standard tools such as routers, so if you're a novice, be sure to practice on scrap wood before you begin.

• If your enthusiasm quells your better judgement, and you end up with a project that doesn't match your garden needs, decor, or space, don't fret. Just turn the finished product into a gift for your most deserving friend.

SAFETY

Many people have a personal, built-in guilt gauge, usually implanted at an early age and triggered into activity when it's exposed to messages that it's heard before and doesn't want to hear again. Messages like "Clean up your room," "Don't talk back," and—the woodworker's favorite—"Don't remove the blade guard from your table saw." Unfortunately, these sensitive mechanisms aren't designed to do anything but register guilt and create poor excuses for ignoring the message itself.

We don't mean to sound unsympathetic, but we're always surprised by how many woodworkers, highly skilled ones at that, depend on these marvels of internal engineering instead of on their common sense. And by how many of these same men and women leave woodworking careers and hobbies minus a finger or eye. Workshop accidents are unnecessary. The next time your guilt gauge kicks on when it's confronted with a basic workshop safety rule, pick up an imaginary hammer, pound the gauge to death, and listen up.

• Why bother to keep your workshop clean and tidy? Because a dirty workshop is a fire hazard, and a messy one can turn into an accident-inviting obstacle course. High on the list of flammable workshop items are oils and finishes. Close the lids of their containers tightly, and store these substances in a cool, dry place; a closed, metal cabinet is ideal. Place finish- or oil-soaked rags in a covered metal container, and empty it often.

• Don't let sawdust accumulate. If you can't afford an exhaust system, open all the windows. Place an ordinary room fan not far from the space in which you do your sawing, and cover its intake side with a furnace filter. This homemade device will collect significant amounts of sawdust for you. Place sawdust sweepings and wood scraps into your lidded, metal trash containers.

• Leave your tobacco habit outside the shop along with your lighter. And make sure that there's an accessible, functional fire extinguisher within easy reach.

• Keep all horizontal surfaces clear of anything that might cause you to slip or that might catch in a moving bit or blade.

• A power tool obeys you, not a set of internally programmed safety rules. If you guide a piece of wood toward its moving parts, it will do its job. It will do the same job, just as efficiently, if you guide careless hands, long hair, or shirt sleeves toward its blade or bit, so stay alert, wear close-fitting clothes, and tie back or tuck up your locks before you start work.

• Blade guards are one of the most important safety devices in any workshop. Keep them in place, and never stand behind or in front of a moving blade, even when the guard is where it should be. Fast-moving blades can catapult wood chips at remarkable speeds.

• If your tools aren't double-insulated, ground them. And unless you've always harbored a secret fascination with electrocution, avoid using them when you're anywhere near standing water. Make sure that cords aren't frayed, and unplug tools whenever you adjust them or change their bits or blades.

• More insidious than the dangers posed by the careless use of tools are those present in your workshop air. When you're working with volatile substances, head outdoors when the weather is pleasant, or use an exhaust fan in your shop when it isn't. No matter where you're working, wear a respirator that's designed to filter out noxious fumes. A dust mask won't work, though it will keep airborne sawdust particles out of your lungs.

• Wear ear plugs or protectors when you use power tools with high volume levels: saws, routers, and the like. Protect your eyes with goggles; woodworkers who use them enjoy good eyesight for many more years than woodworkers who don't.

• Working when you're tense, tired, or upset is self-defeating. Only when they're calm and rested will your body and mind function as one team instead of two in competition. If you're in the mood to strangle your boss, do it before you walk through the workshop door, not after. Your project can wait.

• There's no reason why children can't learn to work with wood, but if you plan to teach them yourself, set your own projects aside and focus on theirs. Eager offspring need your undivided attention in the shop; when you can't pay them that attention, keep them at least one bolted door away from the work space and everything in it.

TOOLS, TECHNIQUES, AND MATERIALS

For those of you whose woodworking skills are rusty or nonexistent, this chapter offers descriptions of all the tools and materials required for the projects in this book, as well as explanations of simple woodworking terms and techniques. By the time you've finished reading it, you'll have learned how to

• share "shop talk" with your woodworking friends

• select a wood that's suitable for your project

• identify and handle the tools required to build it

• apply an appropriate finish to your completed project

• fasten it to a vertical surface if mounting is required

Rather than wade nonstop through every page, you might want to treat this chapter as a thumb-through guide instead. How will you know which sections to read? Just refer to the lists and instructions that accompany your selected project; they'll tell you exactly which tools and supplies are required and which construction techniques you'll be using. Then consult the applicable entries here.

Remember, though, that good woodworkers never stop actively learning. Those who have some experience may want to browse through this material anyway, if only to brush up on techniques that are often taken for granted. Besides, comparing your own methods with those of other woodworkers is a great way to refine and perfect your own techniques.

TOOLS

One assumption that beginners often make is that expensive tools can transform a poor woodworker into a good one. Big mistake! When you set off to purchase equipment for your workshop, remind yourself that the real value of any tool is determined by you—not by its manufacturer. A high-ticket table saw that intimidates you is worth a lot less than a crosscut saw that's user-friendly. When you purchase tools, you'll always want to invest in the best ones you can afford, of course, but keep in mind that a good woodworker can make a few modest tools work miracles.

Remember, too, that modest doesn't necessarily mean cheap. Shoddy tools won't work well, may expire just after their warranties do, and are sometimes even unsafe. If you'll be using a tool only once or twice, don't skimp when you buy; just rent or borrow instead. Look after all tools carefully: clean them, keep them rust-free, check electrical cords, and follow the manufacturers' instructions regarding their use, maintenance, and repair.

By the way, don't discard the instructional pamphlets that come with new tools. Manufacturers have a vested interest in keeping you happy and whole, so the information that they offer is almost certainly accurate. What's more, if you throw these inserts away before you've had a chance to practice with your new purchase, you may miss out on their most useful tips—the ones that never make much sense until you really understand the tool's structure and function.

With any new tool, put in some serious practice time. Get to know its heft, shape, parts, and method of operation. Scrounge for some scrap wood, and try out every one of the tool's functions on it. Wood is no longer inexpensive; you don't want your brand-new tool to acquaint you with its quirks while you're working on a wallet's worth of costly redwood. Besides, there's nothing more frustrating than pulling out a jigsaw or drill for the first time—one that you purchased months ago—only to discover that it's not working properly and its warranty has expired.

Workbench

Yes, a workbench is a tool as far as we're concerned and is one of the most important in your shop. Without it, you'd have no level surface on which to measure, glue, drill, and chisel, and your vise would be without a home. For comfort and working ease, make sure that your bench is hip-height.

One feature of a good workbench is that it's really solid; the heavier it is, the less likely it will be to shift as you work. The stability of your bench will depend largely on its design, but you can minimize the risk of a restless bench by placing it against a solid wall. If movement is really a problem, just bolt the bench to the floor or wall.

Workbenches of high quality will include dogs (see the Vise section on page 19), a vise, a tool well, and stretchers between the legs for extra support. They'll also have a shelf for tool storage. Before you rush out to buy a bench, take a look at some of the many plans available for ones that you can build yourself.

Tools for Measuring and Marking

No amount of fancy maneuvering with expensive tools will result in a successful project if you haven't measured and marked the pieces carefully and accurately in the first place. In fact, no other stage of the construction process has as much influence on the stages that follow. How well you lay out lengths, angles, and joints will determine how well your project is constructed, so don't gloss over the importance of your measuring and marking tools.

Measuring tools establish length, width, and depth. They're absolutely necessary during project construction, and they're useful when you purchase raw stock, too; wise woodworkers check the actual dimensions of lumber before they buy it.

Marking tools are helpful in locating the lines, points, curves, and angles where you intend to cut, rout, or drill.

Steel Tape Measure

A steel tape is a long, flexible, rolled-up ruler that extends from inside a compact case. These tapes are made in widths between 1/4" and 1" and in lengths from 6' to 25'. A hook on one end of the tape secures that end to the work so that you can stretch the tape out without having to hold its loose end in place. Don't toss the tape away when you notice that this hook jiggles; it's loosely mounted to compensate for its own width when measurements are taken.

Graduations are noted along the tape in 1/16" increments (except for the first 12", which are marked in 1/32" increments). For our projects, a 3/4"-wide, 16'-long, self-retracting rule with a tape-lock button would be your best choice.

Straightedge

You'll use a straightedge for close measuring work and for drawing straight lines. It's nothing more than a steel ruler, 12" to 36" in length. When it's not in use, keep this tool hanging well away from other metal objects that might nick its smooth edges.

Speed Square

A speed square is another carpentry tool and is designed to perform a number of common measuring functions rapidly. This tool has a degree scale and increments along its blades for quick calculations related to stair steps, roof pitches, rafter lengths, and other construction features.

Compass

A compass consists of two legs that are pivoted where they join at the top. One leg has a pointed end, and the other holds a pencil. The tool is used to scribe and transfer radius arcs, circles, and patterns during the layout process.

Try Square

This small (5-1/2" x 8") tool consists of a metal blade placed at right angles to a handle; the blade is marked just like a ruler. It's used to check right angles and to take quick measurements.

Combination Square

The adjustable combination square is similar to a try square, but it's slightly larger, its blade can be moved back and forth perpendicular to its handle, and a 45° shoulder is built into its body. This tool does everything that the simpler try square can do, but it can also serve as a depth and miter gauge. Combination squares that come with a built-in scribing tool are used as marking tools, too.

Framing Square

A framing square is shaped like a large right angle. Its two edges are 16" and 24" long, and each is marked with ruler graduations in 1/8" and 1/16" increments. This tool is usually used in construction carpentry to check for 90° accuracy on a large scale. It's also possible to find angles and to solve trigonometry problems with a framing square, but none of the projects presented in this book will require you to engage in those mental acrobatics.

Protractor

A protractor is a simple tool used to determine angles. It has a head with a flat base and a pivoting arm that is attached to the base. The arm is set to the degree of the angle, which is then indicated on a graduated scale etched into the head.

Level

A level is used to establish whether a framing member is level (if it's horizontal), or plumb (if it's vertical). Small tubes of viscous liquid are set into its frame; an air bubble floats within each tube. By

placing the frame on the object and looking at the position of the bubble, you can determine how far off center the object is. The level's long, thin frame of aluminum or wood houses three bubble vials—two at the end, which are positioned to read for plumb, and one in the center, set to read for level. Carpenter's levels come in 24" and 48" lengths.

Line Level

A line level is similar to the carpenter's level just described. Within its lightweight housing, which is equipped with tiny hooks, is a miniature bubble vial. The function of the tool is to determine—with moderate accuracy—the trueness of a horizontal plane. Nylon line is stretched between two points that are several feet or yards apart, and the tool is then suspended from the line by its hooks.

Chalk Line

A chalk line is a 50' or 100' spool of strong line that is housed in a casing full of colored chalk. When the chalk-impregnated line is extended, it leaves a visible mark on any surface that it touches. A hook on one end of the string fastens at one end of the surface to be marked. The string is then stretched across the surface, and its other end is tied to a nail some distance away. To mark a line, the string is snapped smartly against the surface.

Plumb Bob

This tool is simply a pointed 8-ounce (226.8 g) weight that is suspended from a line 20' or 25' long;

it's used to transfer an overhead point to a point directly beneath it. Just suspend the string from the upper point, and mark the position of the bob below.

Tools for Cutting

What distinguishes the function of one saw from another? The number, pitch, bevel, and angle of teeth on its blade. The more teeth per inch of saw blade (a measurement given in points), the smoother (and slower) the blade's cut will be. Saws with fewer points will make coarser, quicker cuts. A crosscut saw, for example, with perhaps eight teeth per inch, can make rapid cuts across thick lumber. A backsaw, on the other hand, with fifteen teeth per inch, works best for fine joinery work,

You could make many of the projects in this book with hand tools, and you're certainly welcome to construct them that way. But unless you have no job, no children, no pets, and no other time-consuming responsibilities, you'll probably want to execute your cuts with power saws.

Power saws often use what are known as combination blades; these will cut cleanly both with and against the grain of the wood. No saw blade, however, will cut well if its teeth are rusted, bent, or dull. A slit length of old hose, slipped over your handsaw's teeth, will protect the teeth when the saw's not in use. Power-saw blades can be protected by hanging them on a pegboard; don't toss them into drawers where they may be damaged by other metal objects.

Crosscut Saw

A crosscut saw cuts across or against the grain of the wood; you'd use one, for example, to cut a 1-1/2" x 20" length from a 1-1/2" x 24" piece of wood. Though crosscut saw lengths vary, a 26" one will work well for any hand-sawing that you do as you construct these projects. These saws are available with 7 through 12 points per inch, depending on how coarse or fine you wish the cut to be.

Ripsaw

A ripsaw is designed to rip wood by cutting with or along its grain. If, for example, you needed a strip 1" wide and 24" long, you might rip it from a 1-1/2" x 24" piece. Most ripsaws are 26" long and come with 4-1/2 through 7 points per inch. Unless you own a power saw, you'll need both a ripsaw and a crosscut saw; while it's possible to rip (slowly) with a crosscut saw, you can't make a decent crosscut with a ripsaw.

Coping Saw

A coping saw is a hand-held saw that looks like the letter U with a handle. Its very thin, brittle blade is fastened, under tension, between the tips of the U-shaped, steel bow frame, which maintains enough tension on the blade to keep it from breaking. The blade has 10 to 12 teeth per inch. This saw is especially useful for cutting curves and interior shapes;

its frame can be angled away from the blade on curved cut-lines, and the blade can be unfastened at one end, slipped through a hole, and refastened in order to cut out interior shapes. It won't do well on boards thicker than 3/4", however.

Circular Saw

The circular saw, which is driven by a motor but held by hand, is a very popular power tool, especially for construction carpentry. It does have its disadvantages: it's heavy, somewhat unwieldy, and therefore sometimes less than accurate. The typical version has a 7-1/4" blade that can be adjusted to cut at angles between 90° and 45°. When the blade is set to cut at a perpendicular, it penetrates to 2-1/4"; at 45°, that depth is reduced to 1-3/4".

Better-quality circular saws often come with carbide-tipped combination blades, which stay sharper longer than regular blades. Regular blades will work just as well, but you'll need to keep them sharpened and replace them frequently. When your circular saw blades aren't in use, take them off the saw, and store them someplace where their teeth won't be damaged.

Table Saw and Dado Blade

A table saw, which is not hand-held but built into a frame and table, gives more accurate cuts than those that a hand-held circular saw can deliver. On the typical table saw, the blade's arbor (or axle) is held by a pivoting carriage that allows the blade to be raised to a 90° angle and tilted up to 45°. The depth of cut at 90° is 3-1/8"; the cut at 45° is 2-1/8" deep.

Table saws are usually equipped with a 10" carbide-tipped combination blade and have a more powerful motor than the hand-held variety. Compact and portable table saws that use smaller blades, but which have the same features as the larger models, are also available.

Table saws also come with rip fences; these are long, straight pieces that run flat across the saw table's surface, parallel to the exposed blade and adjustable to either side of it. To assure accurate rip cuts, you'll hold your material against the fence as you guide the material into the blade.

A miter gauge, another table saw accessory, rests on the saw table's surface and is adjustable to 45° on either side of a perpendicular midpoint. Its function is to hold the stock at the correct angle as the stock is passed through the blade to make a miter cut.

Leave the blade guard in place while you operate the tool; all modern table saws are equipped with one. The guard stands between you and flying wood chips and can also help to prevent blade kickback, which can cause serious injury. You may encounter a situation in which the saw won't accept a particularly thick piece of work unless the guard is removed. When this is the case, always refer to the operator's manual before dismantling the guard; it may contain safety warnings that are well worth heeding.

To make notches and wide grooves, a special cutting tool known as a dado blade is fitted to the table saw. These blades come in two common designs. One consists of an offset blade that wobbles to the right and to the left as it revolves. The other design makes use of two outer blades and a number of inner chippers that are stacked to establish the width of the cut.

Jigsaw
The hand-held jigsaw (or its close cousin the sabre saw) is the power-driven alternative to a coping saw; it cuts curves, shapes, and large holes in panels or boards up to 1-1/2" in thickness. The narrow, reciprocating bayonet blade, which moves very rapidly, is surrounded by a shoe that can be tilted 45° to the right and left of perpendicular for angled cuts.

High-quality jigsaws have a variable speed control and an orbital blade action that swings the blade's cutting edge forward into the work and then back again, through the blade's up-and-down cycle. To keep the cuts clear of sawdust, the saw is designed to incorporate a dust-blower, and the tool may be equipped with a circle-cutting guide and rip fence as well.

Utility Knife
Here's a tool that anyone can afford and everyone should own. It's used to cut thin wood and other materials and to scribe lines for marking. Purchase a

model with a retractable blade and a convenient blade storage pocket in its handle.

Tin Snips
These are just heavy-duty scissors that will cut hardware cloth, wire screen, and sheet metal. They range in size from 8" to 12", with blades up to 4" in length.

Tools for Clamping and Holding
It's not easy to mark, drill, or cut a piece of wood that isn't held securely in place. Fortunately it's not usually necessary, either. To grip parts to each other or to a bench so that they won't shift while you work on them, you'll use clamps. These tools also serve to hold glued parts together as the glue dries. In addition, when they're used in combination with strips of wood, clamps can be transformed into saw and router guides or extended over large areas. Of the many types of clamps manufactured, the only ones you'll need for these projects are C-clamps and bar or pipe clamps.

C-Clamps
C-clamps, aptly named for the C shape of their steel or iron frames, are generally fairly small. One end of the C—the anvil—doesn't move at all. The other end is fitted with a threaded rod and swivel pad. Whatever is placed between the anvil and the threaded end is gripped when the threaded end is tightened. To protect your work from marks left by the clamp's jaws, place rubber pads or pieces of

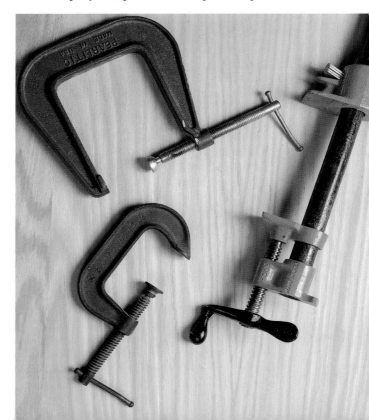

scrap wood between the project wood and metal jaw before tightening the tool down.

C-clamps come in a variety of styles and sizes; woodworking C-clamps are usually limited to a 12" jaw opening. For almost all of the projects in this book, the 6" size will suffice. Though these tools can't span great distances (a bar or pipe clamp serves that purpose), they're perfect for holding narrow pieces of stock together or for clamping work near the edge of the bench. Deep-throated C-clamps will also allow you to apply pressure to the work piece at some distance from its edge.

Bar and Pipe Clamps

Unlike C-clamps, these clamps will span long or wide pieces of wood and can also grip together several pieces of wood that are placed edge-to-edge. (You'll find them useful, for instance, when gluing together the components of the Footbridge or the Two-Seater Bench.) Their frames are simply steel or aluminum bars or sections of iron plumbing pipe that are several feet in length. At one end of the bar or pipe is a fixed head, equipped with a short, threaded rod and a metal pad. At the other end is a sliding tail-stop that can be locked at any position along the bar or pipe in order to accommodate the work.

Pipe clamps are less expensive than bar clamps, but they don't work quite as well. They can, however, be made 6' or more in length. If your budget won't bear the cost of new bar or pipe clamps, purchase pipe-clamp kits instead. These include everything except the pipes themselves, which can be bought and threaded at a plumbing supply store. For our projects, four 48"-long, 3/4" pipe clamps will serve you well.

Vise

A vise is just a bench-mounted clamp, one that's used to hold work pieces together or to hold stock securely while you work on it. A woodworker's vise has smooth, broad jaws, which are usually drilled so that facings can be installed to prevent marring fine work. Better wood vises include a dog; this is a bar that slides up from the movable jaw of the vise to hold work against a similar stop mounted on the bench itself. The dog extends the vise's effective jaw opening by 24" or more. Some vises also make use of a half-nut to provide quick-slide opening and closing; tightening occurs only after the work is in place.

Tools for Drilling and Boring

Boring holes through wood requires the use of drills and bits that are suitable for the particular job. For example, holes can be purely decorative or designed with special features such as a tapered countersink or an internal shoulder.

3/8" Variable Speed Reversible Drill

Although almost any hole can be bored with a hand-operated drill, there's little reason not to own this

inexpensive and versatile tool, which operates more quickly and with less effort than any hand-operated variety. For all the projects in this book, a drill with a 3/8" chuck capacity and a motor amperage of 3.5 amps or greater will do just fine. Cordless versions are available and are appropriate for driving screws and drilling small holes, but they may not be suitable for continuous, heavy-duty work.

We strongly recommend purchasing an electric drill with a variable speed control. This feature allows you to govern the speed of the drill's motor by varying the pressure that you exert on the tool's trigger. A reversible motor is another option, one which will permit you to take screws out just as quickly as you insert them. Both features usually come as a package and are well worth the slight additional expense.

Stop Collar

When you need to control the depth of a drill bit's penetration, use a stop collar. This is a metal (or sometimes plastic) ring that tightens onto the shaft of the drill bit. When the bit sinks into the wood, the collar hits the wood's face and stops the bit from going any deeper. Stop collars are sized to fit different drill-bit diameters.

Countersink

A project's appearance and function can suffer when the head of a screw protrudes above the face of the wood. In order to hide these heads, a countersink is used. This angle-faced bit cuts a shallow, slope-sided hole into the surface of the work, creating a recess in which the head of the screw can rest, flush with the face of the work. A more versatile adaptation of the countersink is described in the next entry.

Specialty Bits

A number of power-drill bits are made to accomplish specific tasks. Forstner bits, for example, are used to drill crisp, flat-bottomed holes; they're made in 1/4" to 2-1/4" diameters. Spade bits bore quickly and make moderately clean holes through wood. They're designed with a center point and two flat cutting edges and come in 1/4" to 1-1/2" diameters.

The bits used most frequently in our projects are countersink/pilot drills (sometimes called screw bits), which combine the hole-drilling and countersinking processes in one operation. The better versions of these bits use what's known as a tapered bit, which follows the contour of a standard wood screw; they also include a stop collar. These combination bits are made for screw size Nos. 5 through 12 and are used in conjunction with a stop collar for most of the projects in this book. This type of drill bit is particularly versatile because it allows the woodworker to countersink a fastener flush with the wood's sur-

face or to counterbore the hole to give the screw a deeper penetration where desirable.

Extension bits—and extension shafts made to fit spade and other types of power bits—allow you to bore holes deeper than a normal-length bit would permit. These bits come in diameters from 3/16" to 3/4" and are usually 18" long. Spade bit extension shafts come in 18" and 24" lengths and are made to fit the standard 5/16" and 7/16" power-bit shanks.

Tools for Chisel and Rout Cutting

Chisel

You'll need only one type of chisel for our projects—the standard mortise chisel. You'll use this cabinetmaker's tool to clean up joints and mortises. A set of four or five bevel-edged chisels for hand or mallet work, in sizes from 1/4" to 1" wide and 7" to 10" long, will be more than sufficient.

In the few projects that require them, you may be working these chisels with a mallet, so if you're purchasing a set, look for better-quality chisels; their handles are reinforced to prevent splitting. If the blades are sharp enough, hand-shaving with these chisels is also possible.

Router

Cutting grooves and rabbets, shaping edges, and making slots are all jobs that can be done with chisels, gouges, rasps, and sanders, but a router will save you

time and frustration. The rounded edges of the Hose Guard project, for instance, were cut with a router and a roundover bit. You could cut and smooth similar edges by hand, but they'd probably end up with visible irregularities, and by the time you'd finished, your temper might be a little uneven, too.

Router bits are held in a collet on the end of a shaft that in turn is supported by a flat base and housing. The shape of the bit determines what type of cut will be made in the work, and handles on the housing allow the operator to control the bit's direction.

The simplest routers have 3/8" collets, external clamp-depth controls, and 6-amp motors. More sophisticated models are known as plunge routers; these allow vertical entry into the work for precise cutting and have 1/2" collets, variable-speed 12- to 15-amp motors, and variable depth controls.

Router Bits
The design and shape of each router bit dictate what form the finished edge or groove in your wood will take. There are over two hundred router-bit styles available for various types of work, but only a few are required for the projects presented here.

When cutting or shaping an edge, a router bit with a ball-bearing pilot at its tip is used. The tip assures a high degree of accuracy in the cut by rolling along the edge of the wood, below the portion being trimmed. Groove- or slot-cutting bits can't use pilot tips, so when you rout a channel, you'll use a guide or temporary fence to guide the tool. The guide clamps onto the tool's base and acts as a moving fence to keep the router and bit following one edge of the work. Either type of bit can be set vertically by adjusting the router base to control the depth of cut.

Tools for Sanding and Smoothing
A piece of wood isn't finished properly unless its surfaces are level and its grain is smooth. Rasps, files, and sandpaper complete these tasks, the first two by cutting away excess material and the last by smoothing the grain and preparing the wood for its final finish.

Rasps and Files
When you need to shape or round a piece of wood, you'll make your first (or rough) cuts with a wood rasp, which is a coarse cutting tool. For finer (or second-cut) work, you'll turn to a cabinet rasp. Both types of rasps are available in three styles: flat on both sides, half-round on one side, and round.

Wood files are not as coarse as rasps and are used for even finer smoothing and finishing work.

They're about 10" long (as are rasps) and usually come in round and half-round cross sections.

For the projects in this book, you're most likely to need only a flat rasp, but it's a good idea to have two grades of files on hand as well. The first, a bastard-cut file, is one step finer than a coarse file. The half-round back on this 10" or 12" tool allows it to be used on inside curves and arcs. The second, a smooth-cut file, is best for finish work. It's the finest of the group and is especially useful in preparing hardwoods for sanding work.

Hand-Sanding Block
If you choose to sand by hand instead of using a power sander, be sure to get yourself a hand-sanding block; it will extend the life of your sandpaper. This simple tool consists of a small, hard rubber piece that fits into the palm of your hand. Sandpaper is placed across its bottom surface and is held securely by some type of clip mechanism at either end of the block.

Sandpaper
Sandpaper and the replaceable pads for palm sanders come in a variety of grits (or degrees of roughness): coarse (No. 60), medium (No. 100), fine (No. 150), and extra-fine (No. 220). Grits in between these are also available.

For woodworking, select standard garnet paper or aluminum-oxide sanding sheets. The garnet paper's abrasive particles continuously break away, exposing fresh material as they do. Aluminum-oxide sanding sheets, however, are more durable and less likely to clog.

Tools for Hammering and Setting

Hammers

The hammer that you'll need for most of these projects is a lightweight tack hammer, 3-1/2 ounces (99.2 g) or 6 ounces (170.1 g) at most. A claw style will do, but what's known as a Warrington hammer is best because, in addition to one traditional flat face, it has one elongated peen for starting the small brads used to secure trim strips.

For the real construction projects like the Footbridge or Gazebo, a 16- or 20-ounce (453.6 g or 567 g) straight-claw framing hammer with a wooden or fiberglass handle is your best choice.

Palm or Pad Sander

Though you're welcome to use a hand-sanding block instead, our projects call consistently for one type of power sander—a palm or pad sander. This hand-held orbital finishing sander has a palm grip and either a round or square pad to which sand-paper is attached. The orbiting mechanism requires a 1-1/2- or 2-amp motor to be effective. For convenience, the round styles make use of self-adhesive paper rather than mechanical clips on their pads.

Spokeshave

A spokeshave is a small, two-handled plane tradi-tionally used for rounding and shaping sharp-cornered edges. It consists of a 2" center-mounted blade, with handles about 4" in length to each side. The handles are drawn toward the user to shave wood from the work.

Nail Set

When you want to sink the head of a finishing nail or brad below the surface of the project, use a nail set. This tool is a punch with a fine point at one end; its purpose is to keep your hammer from marring the surface of the wood. The pointed end is placed on the nail or brad head, and the flat top is tapped with a hammer.

Mallet

Should you need a larger hammer for chisel work or for setting joints, an 8" wooden carpenter's mallet of 12 ounces (340.2 g) or so would do well. Plastic-headed mallets are also useful for this type of work.

Tools for Screw Driving, Stapling, and Tightening

No. 2 Phillips-Head Screwdriver

You'll need a No. 2 Phillips-head screwdriver for almost every project; choose one that's 6" or 8" long, with a molded or wooden handle. This tool will work well on the No. 6, No. 8, and No. 10 screws that the projects require, and its X-shaped head will assure a positive, nearly slipless grip.

Power-Drive Bits

These days, many woodworkers prefer power-drive bits to hand-held screwdrivers. These bits, which alleviate the monotony of sinking screws and speed up the work considerably, are powered by 3/8" variable-speed power drills. Each one has a short, six-sided shank that slips easily into the drill's chuck. The bits come with tips designed for either Phillips-head or slotted screws. Square-drive bits are also available; they drive the newer and increasingly popular square-head screws.

Staple Gun

This hand-operated tool is used for driving staples into softwoods, usually in situations where the fasteners will be covered with a trim strip or will be otherwise invisible. An internal clip holds a row of staples from 1/4" to 7/8" in length, and a spring-loaded mechanism drives a single staple each time you pull the handle.

Adjustable Wrench

As its name implies, this wrench is designed to span a variety of nut and bolt-head sizes. An 8" adjustable wrench can accommodate a hex or square nut from 3/16" to 1" across the face. A knurled thumb-wheel controls and locks the opening of the wrench's jaws.

A Tool For Digging

Post-Hole Digger

This tool consists of two small, semicylindrical shovels that are hinged together at their tops and mounted on the end of two hardwood handles, each about 4' long. The shovels are separated while being driven into the earth and are then forced together with the handles while the earth is being removed. Used correctly, a post-hole digger can excavate a uniform-width hole up to 36" deep.

Techniques

How to Measure and Mark

It should go without saying that careful measurement and layout are the absolute foundations of good woodworking. But we'd like to add one additional maxim: rechecking your measurements will be a waste of time if you used the wrong tool in the first place—your measurements are very likely to have been wrong.

Usually, the steel tape rule is regarded as the backbone of the measuring business. The workaday general measuring jobs fall to this tool because it's both quick and accurate to within 1/16", a perfectly acceptable tolerance for any project in this book.

Don't rely on a steel tape, however, to strike a straight line, particularly over any distance. The metal band will lift, move, or distort no matter how careful you are, and the line will come out curved. And avoid measuring an inside corner with a flexible tape measure; the tape can't be bent sharply enough at the corner to give you an accurate reading. Manufacturers usually mark the outside of the case to indicate its length, but this marked measurement is not often as accurate as your needs will require. To take an accurate measurement along an inside corner, place a square in the corner, and run the tape up to its extended blade; then combine the measurements taken with each.

For distances of more than 3' or 4', a chalk line makes the best marker. For distances less than 36", a straightedge is your best bet; that's why we've recommended it for nearly every project in this book. If necessary, you can use your steel tape to mark 2' increments over greater distances and then strike lines between them with the straightedge. When marking your measured points, a V-shaped pencil mark works best; the point of the V will show you right where to cut.

Establishing a square or perpendicular edge is the square's job; you'll need to use this tool for marking crosscuts or for transferring a line to the remaining three sides of a board. A try square performs this task well on smaller pieces; for larger pieces, use a framing square instead. Press the tool's handle or head against the edge of the work, and mark a pencil line on the work, along the edge of the blade. To transfer that line to the edge and back surfaces of the work, simply "walk" the square around it, using the tail of the previous line as the start of the next one, and so on.

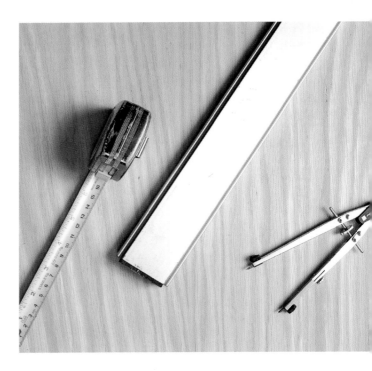

To lay out the radius of a quarter- or half-circle, use the compass. Simply open its legs to the desired radius, place the point at the center of the partial circle or arc you wish to make, and swing the other leg to make the mark. Remember that the radius is half of the width of a circle (or half its diameter), while the diameter is its full width.

Figuring angles can be the bane of us all, but the job isn't quite as intimidating when you own a protractor. The standard transparent or stainless steel half-moon design, with degree graduations along its edge, is adequate for these projects. The protractor's bottom is laid along the baseline of the work, and the measurement is read at the top arc. The more sophisticated bevel protractor has a pivoting arm that can be laid alongside the angle as well, making it easier to read or establish the correct angle or bevel.

A level is used to establish whether or not a member is plumb (straight up-and-down) or level (horizontally even). The level's frame is placed on the side or top of the work piece. The position of the floating bubble within the appropriate vial registers how true the piece is; a centered bubble indicates perfect accuracy. For plumb measurement, the end vials are used. For determining level, the center vial provides the reading.

The line level, a similar tool, hooks onto a string stretched between two points. The string is raised or lowered until the tool's vial shows a centered bubble.

How to Use Clamps

The function of the clamps that you'll be using for these projects is to hold parts together while they're being cut, drilled, or glued. Bar or pipe clamps are especially well suited for oversize clamping jobs because they're so long. Their jaws can stretch to match the width or height of a project, while still maintaining a secure grip.

In the case of joints or pieces less than 12" in depth, C-clamps are logical choices. These clamps come in standard and deep-throat depths, but they all have a threaded rod with a swivel tip that applies pressure to the work as you tighten the rod. To keep the metal tips from marring the face of your work, you may want to use some 2"-square pads cut from scrap pieces of 1/4" plywood.

The best results in piece- or joint-clamping come when you place the clamp's pressure points directly at the centerline of the work or joint to be glued. Snug-tightening is best; over-tightening can damage the wood, and on glued pieces, can force enough adhesive from the joint to weaken it by causing uneven glue distribution.

How to Make Cuts

After you've completed your measuring and marking, making the cuts is simply a matter of following the instructions that come with your project and with the saw that you're using. Your personal safety, especially when power tools are involved, should be a prime concern. Think about what you're going to do before actually doing it. Consider the consequences of each move because once it's made, there's no going back. And please pay attention to what you're doing while you work—the song or sight of a rapidly spinning blade can truly be hypnotic.

When using a handsaw to make a crosscut or rip cut, grip it firmly, but not tensely, with the back of the handle squarely against the ball of your palm. To start the cut, guide the teeth with the outer edge of your thumb, pulling backward so that this first cut is made on an upstroke. Keep the blade square with the wood's surface, and don't forget to start and complete the cut on the waste (or outer) side of the line that you've marked.

For crosscutting, the tool should be held at a 45° angle; rip cuts work better at 60°. Actual cutting pressure should be delivered only on the downstroke.

When using a circular saw, make sure that the blade depth is set so that the teeth penetrate the opposite face of the work fully; to adjust the depth, you'll usually need to loosen a knob or lever and move the shoe up or down. This depth will prevent the blade from jamming. Also, check to see that your sawhorses or supports aren't in the path of the blade, or you'll cut them along with the work.

Assume a comfortable position before starting the saw, one that won't leave you off-balance in a long stretch. Don't grip the handle too tightly, either; doing so will tire your hand and may throw off the accuracy of your work. For extra control, the larger saws come with a second grip at their front end. Two-fisted sawing, however, requires that you clamp your work down firmly before you start to cut.

Draw the power cord behind you before starting the saw, always wear safety glasses, and sight your line of cut along the mark on the front of the saw's shoe. The safety guard will swing up by itself as you move forward. A combination blade with a circular saw will enable you to make either rip cuts or crosscuts.

A table saw allows more precise cutting because it has a cutting fence and a miter gauge. Set the cutting depth with the handwheel located at the front of the saw cabinet; the blade should penetrate the work deeply enough so that several full teeth are exposed during the cut. This depth allows the sawdust to escape and the blade to cool.

To adjust the fence, loosen the lock and slide the fence to the right or left as needed. You can use the gauge on the fence rails for measuring the width of your cut, but a more accurate method is to take a steel-tape reading between the fence's edge and the tip of a blade tooth that is set toward, not away from, the fence.

After starting the motor, give it a few seconds to come up to speed; never shove a piece of wood into a slowly moving blade. And don't put your hands near the spinning blade, either; use a push stick to pass the work through. A kickback or a quick stall can put your fingers right into the saw's teeth, often leaving the work right where it is.

Curve-cutting isn't difficult if you've marked your cutting line clearly. Because it's easy to control, the thin-bladed coping saw is the basic curve-cutting tool for thinner material and for tight contours. If the stock is more than 3/8" or so in thickness, or the line is longer than the throat depth of the saw, a hand-held electric jigsaw is more accurate and easier to use. The tighter the curve or circle, the thinner the jigsaw blade should be; blades that are too thick are likely to bind or overheat, warping the steel and affecting the straightness of the saw kerf (the narrow slot that's being cut).

Cutting at an angle, as when making miters and bevels, can be done in several ways. For clarification, a miter is an angle-cut made across the face of a board (its width); picture frames are miter cut. A bevel is an angle cut into the edge of a board (its thickness); trim or molding is bevel cut. And a compound cut is a combination of both.

For bevel cutting, the shoe on a circular saw can be adjusted to a 45° angle. Similarly, the table saw's blade carriage can be pivoted to the same degree by using the handwheel on the saw cabinet's side.

For manual miter cutting on wood that is less than 6" or so in width, a miter box will be a great help. Held freehand, a backsaw or a larger crosscut saw can do well if the line is clearly marked.

To make a miter cut on the table saw, simply loosen the knob on the miter gauge, and adjust and tighten its small fence at the desired angle. The work is held against the fence, and the gauge (which slides within a slot built into the table) and the work are moved forward toward the blade.

Rabbets and grooves can be cut with a table saw fitted with a dado blade, but with many projects, it's easier to make them using a router and a straight bit. To use the saw for this purpose, remove the table insert, and set the dado-head width; how you do this will depend upon the blade design. The offset wobbler type has a rotating hub that changes the width by altering the degree of offset. The stacked type must be set up out of the saw and reinstalled on the arbor. When you stack the chippers between the outer blades, make sure that the teeth rest between the gullets of the adjacent blades and the chippers are staggered around the circumference. Once the width is established, adjust the blade's depth with the handwheel. Set the fence to establish the rabbet's width as the work is passed through the saw.

Dado grooves for inserts or lattice are saw-cut by running the edge of the frame piece through the blade after the blade has been adjusted for proper width and depth.

How to Make Grooves, Joints, and Edges

On a few of these projects—such as the Boot Bench, which makes use of mortised hinges—you'll need to clean up or straighten surfaces that haven't been completely cut with a saw or router. This is a job for the chisel, and it's really not difficult as long as you maintain the tool's sharp edge.

On most work, you won't even need a mallet. Hold the chisel in your right hand to provide the driving effort, and control the direction of the blade with the left. If you do use a mallet, strike the tool lightly in order to avoid taking big bites. Work with the grain, and whenever possible, hold the tool at a slight angle (right or left); this position provides the smoothest cut and is less likely to dull the blade. To avoid gouging the work, don't drive the edge too steeply. Instead, hold the blade level or at a slight downward angle.

For cuts deeper than a hinge mortise requires—a half-lap joint or a rounded-over edge, for example—the router can accomplish more quickly and cleanly what would normally be a tedious job with a saw, file, or chisel. Only five router bits are required for the projects in this book: 1/4" and 1/2" straight bits, 1/4" and 3/8" roundover bits, and a 3/8" cove bit. The shape of the router bit's cutting surfaces determines what the finished edge or groove will look like. A straight bit makes a slot the width of the bit itself; likewise, a roundover bit cuts a clean, rounded edge into what was a square-ended surface.

When operating a router, grasp it comfortably with both hands, and wear safety glasses so that you can maintain a clear view of the working bit! The rule of thumb is to move the bit from left to right; if circular or irregular cutting is required, then the motion should be counterclockwise. To avoid chipping, first make any cuts across the end grain of your work; then cut with the grain.

The base of the router can be loosened and the motor housing adjusted up or down to control the depth of cut. Before making any permanent cuts, we highly recommend that you run a test on a piece of scrap wood to see what your work will look like. If nothing else, practice will improve your control of the tool, and after a while, you'll no longer need to test every cut before you make it. Instead, you'll be able to rely on the depth gauge marked on the router's side.

Freehand work is fine for short jobs or when the bit is equipped with a pilot bearing, but to keep the cut consistent when cutting long dadoes and grooves, you'll probably need to clamp the wood to a bench and use the tool's base-mounted straight guide. If you don't have a guide, you can usually create a substitute by clamping a straight section of 1 x 2 to the bench or work, alongside and parallel to the line of cut.

When mortising narrow stock or edge-rabbeting grooves, place a piece of scrap stock to the right and left of the work, flush with the working surface. This will prevent the router base from tilting to one side and spoiling the cut; it will also give you a place to mount a guide if you use one.

How to Drill Holes

A wood-screw hole consists of three parts: the pilot, or lead, hole, which is a little more than half the diameter of the screw itself; the shank hole, which is the same diameter as the screw; and the sink or bore, which is necessary if the screw head is to be recessed below the surface of the wood.

In softwoods, it's not really necessary to drill more than just the pilot hole; even then, it's sunk only a little more than half the length of the screw in order to give the threads a better bite.

Very dense hardwoods and long screws may require that you drill the shank hole, too. Make that hole only as deep as the shank (the unthreaded portion of the screw) is long. Also, it's worth noting that screws driven into wood's end-grain have less than half the holding power of a screw driven perpendicular to the grain.

Combination countersink/pilot bits simplify hole-drilling considerably. They're sized by screw numbers, and their stop collars and countersinks are adjustable for length. The versions called screw-bits are tapered to accommodate standard wood screws perfectly.

Where appropriate (in softwoods, for No. 6 and No. 8 screw diameters), self-tapping, power-driven screws—sometimes called drywall or cabinet screws—are even more convenient, though you should take care to predrill pilot holes when driving these screws near the end of the wood. We've called for a third variation known as deck screws in almost all of the projects. If possible, choose the brass-colored type; these screws are coated with a smooth anodization that makes them weather-resistant. They'll work in hardwoods as well, but always predrill the screw holes, or you'll run the risk of splitting the wood or shearing the screw head off when the fastener is driven in place.

Boring sockets for dowels can be done with a regular drill bit if the diameter of the bit is small enough—1/4" or 3/8". To bore a larger hole, use a spade bit, or better yet, a Forstner bit, which produces a clean, flat-bottomed hole. A stop collar can be used on a standard drill bit if you feel you might have trouble gauging the depth of a socket accurately.

In order not to tear out the back side of your work, you'll need to drill through-holes and bores with care, especially if another piece is planned to face it. Here's a technique that will help you to avoid splintering wood this way. Begin by drilling only part of the way through the piece. Then use a small pilot bit, inserted through the partial bore, to mark a point on the back by barely penetrating it. Finally, complete the bore from the back, using the original bit.

How to Glue and Fasten

Using the screw fasteners called for in these projects doesn't require any special technique other than setting the stop collar for the correct depth when drilling the pilot holes. The depth set-up for the screws in all the projects has been clearly indicated in the construction procedures; it takes into account the counterbore needed for flush-mounted screws (a feature that is the rule throughout all the projects), and in joints and surfaces that will be exposed, allows for a wood buffer beyond the point of the screw.

One word of caution: Softwoods have a tendency to give, and power drivers can sink a screw farther and faster than you might think. Avoid driving screw points through the back surfaces of exposed joints!

With hardwoods especially, don't over-tighten fasteners, or you may spin off the screw heads or split the joints. The wood will swell slightly as it absorbs indigenous moisture, and swollen wood will make joints even tighter. In the projects that call for brads, you can avoid splitting the wood by using a small-diameter drill bit to predrill the holes. This is an especially useful technique when you're driving brads close to the end of the wood.

We've recommended using a tack hammer for brads because of the control it offers. If you use a larger hammer, in the 12- to 16-ounce (340.2 g to 453.6 g) range instead, be careful not to bend the brad's wire body or drive it in at an extreme angle. And with any hammer, don't miss your mark, or you'll mar the wood and, if you're really unlucky, your fingers as well.

When setting a brad, use the smallest nail set practical. Drive the head of the brad just below the wood's surface.

To give glue the best chance to work, make sure that the surfaces to be joined are dry and free of loose material and surface oils. They should also meet flush to each other because the aliphatic resins that we recommend are not intended to fill gaps. This glue should be used at a temperature above 55˚F (approximately 13˚C) so that the resins will soak deeply into the wood's grain and the proper chemical reaction will occur. Once it has dried, this type of glue will be visible, so be sure to wipe excess glue from all finished surfaces while the glue is still wet.

Aliphatic resins set up in less than an hour and are fully cured in twenty-four hours. Coat both joining surfaces with a liberal application of glue, and then clamp the pieces together. Don't over-tighten the clamps, or you'll force so much glue from the joint that there won't be enough left on the wood to do its job.

How to Fasten the Mounted Projects

A few of the projects in this book are meant to be fastened to a wall or attached to a railing. This section provides some guidelines for correctly mounting these racks and box shapes.

You'll probably attach your projects to a garage or shed wall or to a garden wall or fence. If you're fastening something to the side of a building, it pays to locate and use the studs (or vertical framing members), which should be set every 16" or 24" behind the exterior surface of the wall. To find these studs, first look or feel for nail heads or bumps along the siding or sheathing. If you find evenly spaced, vertical rows of bumps, a stud is almost certainly standing behind them. If this method doesn't work, magnetic and electronic stud-finders are available at home-improvement centers; they'll locate the studs for you. When you're attaching the project to a

fence, the structural parts—posts or top rails—will be obvious.

Ideally, the projects should be mounted with No. 6 or No. 8 deck screws of a length that will penetrate the support by at least the thickness of the project's mounting board or a minimum of 3/4". Predrill the holes in the project, using a countersink bit with the stop collar set so that the head of the screw is just flush with the wood's surface. Use brass screws for a more finished look.

When you need to mount the project on a frame wall, space the screws to match the center-to-center distance between the studs. On projects narrower than 16", you'll have to use one screw in the project's center and one in line below it.

For mounting a project to a brick wall, use a 1/4" machine-screw expansion shield. First, drill a 1/2" hole into the brick or block, using a hardened masonry bit. The shield, which resembles a lead or metal sleeve, fits into the hole and expands to lock in place when a machine screw is tightened into it. You'll have to use a 1-1/2" flathead machine screw as a fastener in this instance because the standard wood-screw thread won't work.

How to Set a Post

For projects such as the Handy Box, which is mounted on a post, it's important that the required hole be deep enough and that you use the proper tool to dig it. A shovel will certainly get the job done, but it will also disturb the soil around the opening, which weakens the ability of the hole to support the post. A post-hole digger is the tool of choice because it creates a deep, narrow-shouldered hole. A 12" depth should be sufficient for the post-mounted projects, although a hole 18" to 24" is recommended.

Choose a site that complements your project, and be sure that there are no footings, drainpipes, or utility lines buried beneath your intended site. Excavate the hole and set the dirt to one side, nearby. To ensure good drainage, place an inch or so of coarse gravel into the bottom of the hole. Then place the post into the hole, and use a level to take a reading on two adjacent sides of the post. Backfill the earth evenly around the post, and tamp the earth down with a 2 x 4.

None of the post-mounted projects needs to be set in concrete. But if you're concerned about stability, you can always drive a few 16d nails into the sides of the post below ground level.

MATERIALS

Fasteners

For the sake of convenience, our projects rely on only a few types of fasteners. No. 6 flathead Phillips screws, 1-1/4" in length, are widely used, as are No. 8 flathead Phillips screws 1-1/2" long. A longer No. 10 screw is used in places where deep penetration is required for strength.

You'll notice that many of these projects require the use of deck screws. This type of screw fastener has two advantages over traditional flathead slotted wood screws. First, these screws are designed to be used with a power driver, which makes their installation easier; drywall screws have this same advantage. Second, deck screws have a special coating—either galvanized or anodized—that makes them especially weather-resistant.

Brads (wire nails) serve to fasten narrow joints and trim. The 16-gauge x 1-1/4" finish brad is used to secure strips and butt joints that aren't under a lot of stress.

The other nails used are for construction projects. 16d commons hold framing members together, as do the lighter and shorter 8d version. 6d casing nails are for trim pieces. The roofing and concrete nails are for specific and self-explanatory uses.

Machine screws—which include carriage bolts and anything else that uses a nut to secure a part—are more substantial than wood screws; the washer and nut prevent "pullout" on a stressed joint. A nutted thread also allows parts to pivot easily.

Wire staples are used to secure hardware cloth, mesh, poultry wire, and screen. The heavier the gauge (or thickness) of the wire (lower numbers represent heavier material), the more substantial the staple needs to be. The No. 5 x 3/8" staples used in the Soil Sifter, for example, are hammered in place. Smaller staples for window screen—as in the Drying Rack—are "shot" in place with a hand-held, spring-loaded staple gun.

Glues and Adhesives

Only one type of wood glue is needed for our projects: a nontoxic, waterproof wood glue. The pre-catalyzed aliphatic resin now on the market offers the advantages of standard yellow carpenter's glue (ten- to forty-five-minute setting and twelve- to twenty-four-hour curing), but resists the effects of water and weather. If this type of adhesive isn't available, a more costly two-part resorcinol can be used, though it takes about twelve hours to set and at least another twelve to cure completely.

Finishes

For almost every project, we've selected wood species for their rot-resistance and for their visual enhancement of a project's appearance. Because these species are attractive in themselves, we

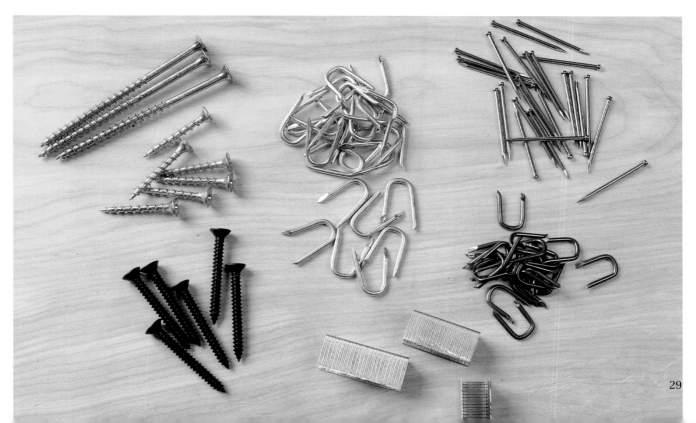

haven't suggested that you stain the wood before applying a top-coat finish. Though none of the recommended species (except for pine) needs a finish, by all means use one if you feel that doing so will add that individual touch to your project.

A finish will protect the wood while still allowing it to adjust to humidity and temperature. On many of these outdoor projects, we've suggested the application of a clear wood finish, which is the finish that's used to protect decks, railings, and other wooden parts of a house left exposed to the weather.

Clear wood finish is available from a number of manufacturers, either as an oil-based or as a waterborne product. It's commonly referred to as a waterproofing agent or as a water repellent to be used after refurbishing weather-worn wood. Its actual appearance can vary from a smooth, semigloss sheen to a dull, almost imperceptible finish. Clear wood finish can be applied by brush or roller or sprayed on under pressure.

Apply this finish in a well-ventilated area; too much exposure to the vapors can be harmful. Some water-borne products are available with reduced Volatile Organic Compounds (VOCs), the irritating vapors that are released at room temperatures. A few manufacturers specifically market these reduced-VOC products for health-conscious individuals, and they're available if you take the time to search for them.

Tung oil is a natural oil pressed from tung nuts; it dries to a mildly durable and flexible finish. If possible, tung oil should be applied warm. Pour it onto the wood, and wipe the wood immediately with a clean cloth. Don't let the oil start to dry, or it may become sticky. Give the wood several applications, according to the label instructions, and allow adequate time (at least eight hours) for drying before you put the project to use.

Paints are a matter of preference. Any of our projects are suitable for painting, but it would be a shame to cover their natural grain without a good reason! If you do choose to paint, make sure that the wood is well sanded and free of dirt and oils. For the sake of your health and ease of clean-up, it's probably best to use a latex (or water-based) paint.

Buy a good-quality, 1-1/2" synthetic brush, and practice spreading the paint using long, even strokes—in one direction. Apply a primer coat first to seal and level the grain; then, once that coat is dry, give the wood a first coat. When that has dried, apply the final coat of paint.

Pigmented or semitransparent stains, which are usually brushed on like paint, are often used on decks as a substitute for expensive deck paints. Because they're pigmented, they impart some color to the wood. They're not only economical, but tend to soak into the grain and therefore last longer than regular paint. When you use pigmented stain products, remember that the color can settle to the bottom of the container if the stain isn't stirred regularly during the application process. Pigmented stains are usually alkyd-based and often contain a wood preservative of some type.

Wood

Wood is appealing, warm, and workable—all excellent reasons for its popularity as a building material. But wood also has characteristics that can be a bit intimidating to those who aren't familiar with them.

Wood products are sold according to the use for which they're intended. The projects in this book are constructed entirely of softwoods, most types of which should be available from a local lumberyard or from a home-improvement center. Unless you happen to live close to an area in which they grow, the less common species (cypress, and in some locations, redwood) may have to be ordered through a sawmill operation or specialty supplier.

If you're fortunate enough to live near a source of wood, a private sawmill can be a real boon. The operator will probably be able to get you any species that grows within 100 miles; alternatively, you can bring the sawyer your own logs for cutting. Also, sawyers sometimes swap with others in different locations in order to lay in a supply of something unusual to their own area; it's not unheard of to get swamp cypress from a mill in the inland mountains. Prices, of course, will vary according to quality and demand.

Extractives in the wood yield the properties of color, density, strength, and so forth. All softwood and hardwood categories are based on these elements.

Broadly speaking, commercial softwoods such as pine and cedar are readily available, reasonably priced, and easy to work with. Strength is not a factor for the projects in this book; any clear-grade softwood is acceptable. Pressure-treated lumber, of course, is a standard yard item and is often available at sale prices.

The specialty softwoods—cypress and redwood—are generally considered to be higher quality woods; they're more expensive and not as available. Redwood is stronger and somewhat more attractive than the other softwood species.

Unless you have access to a custom sawmill, the wood you purchase will meet the standards of the industry. Commercial softwoods are sized and priced by their rough mill-sawn dimensions. But when the raw stock is planed down, as it needs to be in the marketplace, its overall size can be reduced by as much as 25%. When you shop for lumber, you may come across the term nominal, which refers to the original sawn dimension. After a piece of wood has been planed down, it's sold at its actual dimension. Hence a nominal 1 x 2 actually measures only 3/4" x 1-1/2". (The Softwood Sizes chart on page 144 provides both nominal and actual dimensions.)

Softwood less than 1" thick and between 2" and 6" wide is called a strip; wood less than 2" thick and up to 16" wide falls into the board category. Standard lengths run from 6' to 16', in two-foot increments.

Wood is sold in volume by the board foot, a long-standing measure by which each unit is equivalent to a rough board measuring 1" thick x 12" wide x 12" long—144 cubic inches all told. By the rule, any stock less than an inch thick is counted as a full inch, and anything over 1" is figured to the next larger 1/4". So, a 6'-long 1 x 6 contains three board feet; so does a piece measuring 1-3/8" x 2" x 12'. To figure board feet, multiply thickness by width in inches, and then multiply by length in feet and divide by 12.

Lumber is categorized, or graded, by a variety of physical standards and then further by use, according to standards established with help from the softwood manufacturing associations. Appearance, cost, and species are likely to be your main concerns when you shop for project wood.

Softwoods, including pine, will be graded as either finish or select. The select grades, which include shelving and trim stock, are B & Better (commonly known as 1 and 2 Clear), and C Select, which contains limited defects.

Check the wood visually before you buy it. Some lumberyards try to discourage hand-picking, so be prepared not to pay for something that doesn't meet your standards. Watch for knotholes, surface imperfections, warpage, and checks or cracks. In specialty woods, where you're paying for appearance, be especially critical of pith (soft spots), stain, and insect holes.

Don't be overly concerned about the wood's workability. Every species we've recommended will cut cleanly with sharp tools, and redwood is especially easy to work. Cedar, however, has a tendency to split.

Making a final decision about which woods to use may be a simple matter of economics; a pickup load of cedar may be worth more to you than a few arm-loads of redwood.

A FINAL WORD

As you read through the Suggested Tools and Hardware and Supplies lists that accompany your selected projects, you'll notice that they include only the most relevant items. You'll always need marking tools such as pencils, for instance, and workshop supplies like rags, even if you don't find them on the lists. The one way to make sure that you have everything you need—and build something that you'll really enjoy—is to read the instructions thoroughly before you start. Play out each step in your mind before you begin. Make a list of every tool that you see yourself using, and before you start the construction process, find the answers to any questions you might have. Preparation time is always time well spent.

THE PROJECTS

Gardening goals are as varied as the gardeners who have them. Some folks (and perhaps you're one of them) can't stop dreaming of outdoor organization. Their fantasy yards come complete with straight rows and paths, symmetrical flower beds, and manicured lawns. This energetic group will like the projects that are tailored to create order from chaos: a file box for seeds, a boot bench, a tool tote, and more.

Perhaps you're a more relaxed outdoor type. If your imaginary backyard is filled with wild flowers, small, furry animals, and meandering streams, you'll probably enjoy the garden bench, squirrel whirler, and foot-bridge—projects designed for lazy days and leisure.

Other gardeners aim for elegance. Their daydreams tend toward grand estates, ringed by clipped hedges and dotted with formal herb beds. While none of these projects will increase your outdoor acreage, the gazebo, garden gong, and sundial will add a touch of class to it.

And then there are the simpler dreams. Just enough crisp lettuce to satisfy the family *and* the resident rabbits. A yard that's pretty even when the grass isn't mowed. A sunny spot for a quiet cup of morning coffee. If you're a down-to-earth gardener, you'll definitely want to build the compost bin, seedling tray, and picnic table for two.

No matter what your garden looks like now or what you'd like it to be, these projects will help you to transform longed-for landscapes into real pleasures. So, welcome—all of you—to the wonderful world where woodworking and gardening meet.

FIREWOOD BRACE

Some people really enjoy braving winter blizzards to haul their firewood indoors each day. We don't. Instead of stacking logs indoors, where insects in the wood might damage our home, we keep this firewood brace in a sheltered spot just ten paces from our back door—a quick trip with no risk of frostbite, even when the weather's less than pleasant.

Suggested Tools

Table saw
3/8" Drill
No. 8 Pilot bit and countersink with stop collar
Jigsaw
Compass
Tape measure
Try square
No. 2 Phillips screwdriver
Palm sander

Cut List

Cedar or pressure-treated lumber is recommended for this project.

4	Legs	3/4" x 5-1/2" x 36"
2	Side supports	3/4" x 5-1/2" x 48"
4	End supports	3/4" x 5-1/2" x 24"
8	End slats	3/4" x 2-1/2" x 25-1/2"
8	Bottom slats	3/4" x 5-1/2" x 24"

Hardware and Supplies

Waterproof wood glue
No. 8 x 1-1/4" Deck screws
No. 8 x 1-1/2" Deck screws
Exterior clear wood finish

Construction Procedure

1. Fasten the two 24" lower end supports to the ends of the 48" side supports with glue and No. 8 x 1-1/4" deck screws. Use a No. 8 pilot bit to drill three holes at each joint, and set the stop collar at 1-1/4". Space the holes 1-3/4" apart.

2. Fasten one 24" bottom slat to each end of the frame just completed so that their edges are flush with the ends of the frame. Use glue and No. 8 x 1-1/2" deck screws. The screws should be flush-

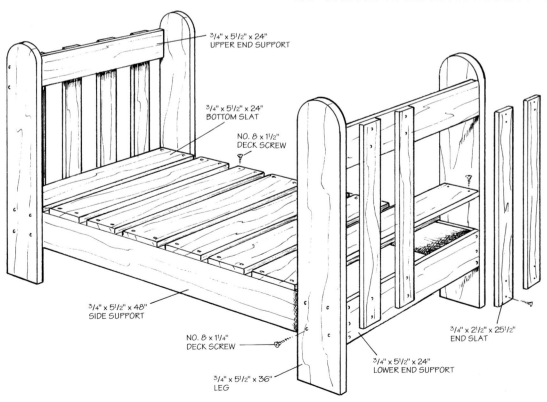

3/4" x 5¹/2" x 24"
UPPER END SUPPORT

3/4" x 5¹/2" x 24"
BOTTOM SLAT

NO. 8 x 1¹/2"
DECK SCREW

3/4" x 5¹/2" x 48"
SIDE SUPPORT

NO. 8 x 1¹/4"
DECK SCREW

3/4" x 5¹/2" x 36"
LEG

3/4" x 2¹/2" x 25¹/2"
END SLAT

3/4" x 5¹/2" x 24"
LOWER END SUPPORT

mounted; drill all holes using a pilot bit with the stop collar set at 1-1/2". Attach the remaining six bottom slats between the two already mounted, leaving about 7/8" between all slats.

3. Find the centerline of each of the 36" legs at one end. Measure down 2-3/4" on each centerline, and mark. With a compass, and using these points as centers, mark a 2-3/4" radius at the end of each leg. Then use a jigsaw to cut along the curved lines. At the opposite end of each leg, mark 6" from the end, and draw a line across the board with a square. Fasten each leg to a side corner so that the 6" mark lines up with the lower edge of the support frame. Check with a square. The legs should be glued and fastened with No. 8 x 1-1/4" deck screws. Place the screws in a square pattern, spacing them 3-1/2" apart.

4. Measure up 28" from the bottom of each leg, and mark on the inside face. Fasten a 24" upper end support between the legs at each end so that its lower edge is even with the marks just made. At each joint, use a No. 8 pilot bit to drill two holes 3-1/2" apart. Glue and fasten with No. 8 x 1-1/4" deck screws.

5. Fasten four 25-1/2" end slats vertically between the upper and lower supports at each end of the brace, using glue and No. 8 x 1-1/4" deck screws. The spacing between each piece—including the two legs—should be 2-13/16". The upper edge of each slat should be flush with the top edge of the upper end support. Predrill the holes with a No. 8 pilot bit, and set the stop collar at 1-1/4".

6. Sand any rough grain from the surface of the brace. No finish is needed for cedar or pressure-treated lumber, but several coats of an exterior clear wood finish will enhance this project's appearance.

BERRY BOX

GATHERING BERRIES IN A PAIL MAY SOUND LIKE FUN,
BUT THE LAST TIME WE TRIED IT, THE BERRIES AT THE
BOTTOM OF THE BUCKET HAD TURNED TO MUSH BY THE
TIME THEY REACHED THE KITCHEN. THE SHALLOW TRAY
IN THIS PROJECT KEEPS THE BERRIES FROM BEING
CRUSHED, BUT IT'S LARGE ENOUGH TO HOLD SIX
QUART-SIZED CONTAINERS.

Suggested Tools

Table saw
3/8" Drill
No. 8 Pilot bit and countersink with stop collar
1" Forstner bit
Jigsaw
Tape measure
No. 2 Phillips screwdriver
Try square
Tack hammer
Nail set
Palm sander

Cut List

Cedar, redwood, or pine is recommended for this project.

Qty	Part	Dimensions
2	Sides	3/4" x 3" x 18"
2	Ends	3/4" x 3" x 12"
1	Center divider	3/4" x 5-1/2" x 16-1/2"
10	Bottom slats	1/4" x 1-5/8" x 13-1/2"

Hardware and Supplies

Yellow wood glue
No. 8 x 1-1/2" Drywall screws
16-gauge x 1-1/4" Finish brads

Construction Procedure

1. To create the finger-hole pattern in the 5-1/2" x 16-1/2" center divider, first locate the center of the piece, and make two marks across the board, 7/16" to the right and left of that point (see Hole Placement). Then measure down 1-3/4" from the top edge, and draw a line crossing the two marks. That done, measure 1-1/4" to the right and left of the centerpoint, and mark. Draw a line through those marks, 1-1/2" down from the top edge.

2. Use a 1" Forstner bit to drill holes at the four places where the lines intersect.

3. To mark the curved upper corners on this board, mark lines 2" in from the top and sides of each upper corner. Using a compass, strike a 2" radius from the points where these lines meet. Cut along the curved lines with a jigsaw, and sand the piece smooth.

4. Locate the center of each end piece, and mark a line across its width. Butt the center divider against the ends, centering it on the marked lines and making sure that the bottom edges of all three pieces are flush. Use the No. 8 pilot bit to drill two holes, 2" apart and 1-1/2" deep, through each end. Fasten the ends to the center divider with No. 8 x 1-1/2" drywall screws.

5. Place the side pieces against the end pieces, checking to see that the bottoms are flush. With the No. 8 pilot bit, drill two holes, 2" apart, at each joint. Fasten each joint with two No. 8 x 1-1/2" drywall screws.

6. Glue and nail two 1-5/8" x 13-1/2" slats to the bottom of the tray, one at each end, so that they're flush at the ends and sides. Use 1-1/4" finish brads to fasten the slats.

7. Attach the remaining eight slats in the same manner, spacing them evenly, about 3/16" apart, between the two already fastened.

8. Sand the entire project. It requires no finish but can be painted if you like.

HOLE PLACEMENT

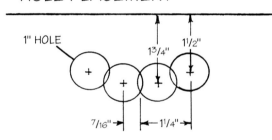

1" HOLE

1³/4"

1¹/2"

7/16"

1¹/4"

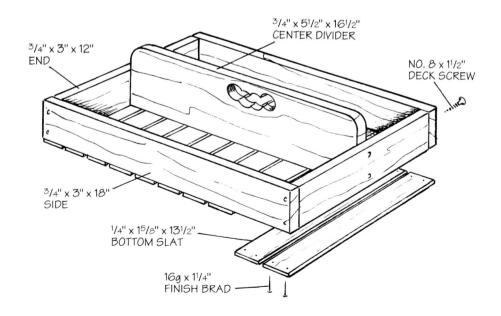

³/4" x 3" x 12"
END

³/4" x 5¹/2" x 16¹/2"
CENTER DIVIDER

NO. 8 x 1¹/2"
DECK SCREW

³/4" x 3" x 18"
SIDE

¹/4" x 1⁵/8" x 13¹/2"
BOTTOM SLAT

16g x 1¹/4"
FINISH BRAD

GARDEN WAGON

THOUGH IT MAY NOT WIN AWARDS FOR ITS LOOKS, THIS PROJECT COULDN'T BE MORE USEFUL TO THE ACTIVE GARDENER. ITS NOTCHED BRACES WILL HOLD STANDARD GARDEN TOOLS, EACH SECTION IS LARGE ENOUGH FOR A BUSHEL BASKET OF COMPOST OR FRESHLY PICKED CORN, AND THE SCREENED BOTTOM KEEPS GARDEN DEBRIS FROM COLLECTING WHERE IT'S NOT WANTED. THE WAGON IS JUST WIDE ENOUGH TO BE WHEELED ALONG A GARDEN AISLE.

Suggested Tools
Table saw
3/8" Drill
No. 8 Pilot bit and countersink with stop collar
3/8" Drill bit
1" and 1-1/4" Spade bits
Jigsaw
Tape measure
24" Straightedge
Compass
Try square
No. 2 Phillips screwdriver
Adjustable wrench
Palm sander
Tin snips
Leather work gloves

Cut List
Cedar or pressure-treated pine is recommended for this project.

2	Sides	3/4" x 3-1/2" x 72"
6	Ends, centers, and end supports	3/4" x 3-1/2" x 18-1/2"
2	Handle extensions	3/4" x 2-1/4" x 24"
1	Handle support	3/4" x 2-1/4" x 20"
1	Axle support	2-1/2" x 2-1/2" x 20"
1	Plywood template	1/2" x 18-1/2" x 23"

Hardware and Supplies
Waterproof wood glue
1" x 21-1/2" Dowel
1/2" x 3" Lag bolts (two)
1/2" Flat washers (four)
7" Replacement lawn-mower wheels (two)
No. 8 x 1-1/2" Deck screws
No. 5 x 3/8" Wire-cloth staples
20-gauge x 1" poultry wire, 24-1/2" x 26" (three)

Construction Procedure

1. Fasten the 72" side boards to two 18-1/2" end boards, using glue and two No. 8 x 1-1/2" deck screws at each joint. Predrill the holes with a No. 8 pilot bit, setting the stop collar at a 1-1/2" depth.

2. Slip one 18-1/2" end support between the sides so that each is flush with the lower edge of the sides and the ends. Fasten these pieces in the same manner, placing five screws, 3-1/2" apart, through each

end board and two screws, 2" apart, through each side.

3. Measure 3/4" in from one edge of each of the two 18-1/2" center boards, and mark a line along each board. On this line, mark points 4" from each end, and one in the center.

4. To make the tool slots, use a 1-1/4" spade bit to drill a hole at each of the marked points, three on each board. Use a try square to square the sides of each opening, and then cut along the marked lines with a jigsaw, creating open slots for the handles of your tools. (If your tools have especially hefty handles, you might want to use a larger bit to make the holes.)

5. Measure 23" and 23-3/4" from each inside end corner of the box, and using the try square, mark lines on each side board. Place the two slotted cen-

ter pieces between opposing sets of marked lines, and glue them in place. Fasten the centers with No. 8 x 1-1/2" deck screws, placed 2" apart.

6. To shape the poultry wire before attaching it, first place each section of wire beneath an 18-1/2" x 23" scrap of 1/2" or 3/4" plywood so that the edges of the wire extend beyond the wood. Next, cut out sections of exposed wire at each corner. Then fold the wire upward at each edge. Finally, keeping the plywood template in place, fold the cut edge of each wire side down evenly toward the outside.

7. Fasten one section of poultry wire into each tray section, flush with the lower edge, and use wire-cloth staples, placed about 3" apart, to fasten the wire to the sides, ends, and centers.

8. Set the miter gauge on the table saw to 28°, and trim one end of each 2-1/4" x 24" handle extension. Measure 1-1/8" from the opposite end, and mark in the center of each board. Using a compass centered at each of these points, scribe a 1-1/8" radius at the end of each extension. Then cut along the lines with a jigsaw.

9. Measure 1-1/4" from the rounded end of each handle extension. At that point, in the center of each piece, use a spade bit to drill a 1" hole. Then, to mark the location of the handle support, measure down 5" and 7-1/4" from each curved end, and mark across the centers of the boards.

10. Glue the 1" x 21-1/2" dowel handle into the 1" holes so that its ends are flush with the outer faces of the extensions. Then position the handle support between the marked lines, and fasten it in place with two No. 8 x 1-1/2" deck screws, spaced 1-1/4" apart, at each end. The holes should be predrilled using a No. 8 pilot bit, with the stop collar set at a 1-1/2" depth.

11. Place the handle assembly at one end of the frame so that the angled cuts on the bottom of the extensions are parallel to the base of the frame and 4-5/8" below it. Using a No. 8 pilot bit, with the stop collar set at 1-1/2", predrill four evenly spaced pilot holes in a square pattern through each extension. Fasten the extensions using glue and No. 8 x 1-1/2" deck screws.

12. Using the blade of a try square, draw lines between opposite corners on each face end of the 20" axle support. With a 3/8" drill bit, bore a pilot hole at the intersecting points. Fasten the wheels to the wooden support using 1/2" x 3" lag bolts, placing flat washers to each side of the wheels.

13. Fasten the axle support to the bottom of the front end support, using glue and three No. 8 x 1-1/2" deck screws. Insert the screws from the top, spacing them 6" apart.

14. Sand the frame and the handle assembly to remove any burrs or splinters. Treated lumber requires no finish, though the wood can be painted if you wish.

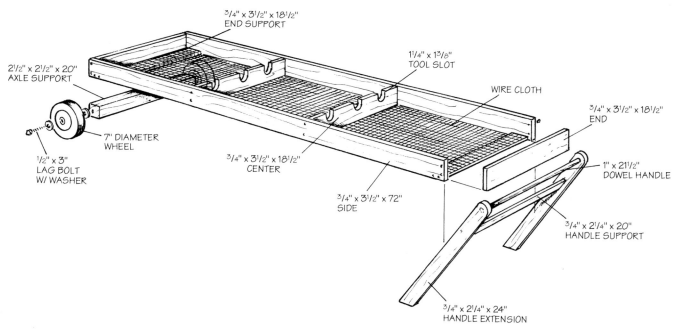

3/4" x 3 1/2" x 18 1/2"
END SUPPORT

1 1/4" x 1 3/8"
TOOL SLOT

2 1/2" x 2 1/2" x 20"
AXLE SUPPORT

WIRE CLOTH

3/4" x 3 1/2" x 18 1/2"
END

7" DIAMETER
WHEEL

1/2" x 3"
LAG BOLT
W/ WASHER

3/4" x 3 1/2" x 18 1/2"
CENTER

3/4" x 3 1/2" x 72"
SIDE

1" x 21 1/2"
DOWEL HANDLE

3/4" x 2 1/4" x 20"
HANDLE SUPPORT

3/4" x 2 1/4" x 24"
HANDLE EXTENSION

TOOL TOTE

❧

If stumbling around the garden with an arm-load of trowels, forks, and clippers isn't one of your greater gardening pleasures, this handy tote is for you. Grab it when you leave the house, plunge its spiked legs into the soil when you need both hands to work, and replace the tools in its small rack or bin when you're through.

TOOL TOTE

Suggested Tools

    Table saw
    3/8" Drill
    No. 8 Pilot bit and countersink with stop collar
    1/2" and 1-1/2" Spade bits
    Router
    3/8" Roundover bit
    Jigsaw
    Compass
    Tape measure
    24" Straightedge
    C-clamps
    Try square
    No. 2 Phillips screwdriver
    Palm sander

Cut List

Cypress is recommended for this project.

1	Center support	3/4" x 5-3/4" x 18"
1	Tool support	3/4" x 2-1/2" x 12"
2	Box sides	3/4" x 2-1/2" x 5-1/2"
9	Slats	1/4" x 3/4" x 5-1/4"

Hardware and Supplies

    Waterproof wood glue
    No. 8 x 1-1/2" Deck screws
    16-gauge x 1-1/4" Finish brads

Construction Procedure

1. Using a straightedge, strike a centerline down the length of the 5-3/4" x 18" center support. Measure and mark a point on the centerline, 4-1/4" from one end. Then use a compass centered at this point to strike a 4-1/4" radius across the top of the support (see Center Support Layout).

2. Measure and mark a point on the centerline, 2-5/8" from the top of the radius. Using this mark as a center-point, strike a 3-1/2"-diameter (1-3/4"-radius) circle.

3. With a jigsaw, cut outside the upper radius. Then use a 1/2" spade bit to drill out the center of the 3-1/2" circle, and remove the circle with the jigsaw.

4. At the opposite end of the center support, measure up 5", and mark on the centerline. Using a compass centered at this mark, strike a 4"-diameter circle with a compass. With a square, extend the edges of the circle to the end of the board.

5. To create legs, cut along the lines and the top of the circle with a jigsaw. Trim the ends of each leg at a 45° angle. If you'd like to round the edges of the center support, do so now, using a 3/8" roundover bit in the router. Sand the wood smooth.

6. To locate the position of the tool support, strike a line 5" down from the top of the arc on the center support; use a square to do this.

7. Strike a centerline lengthwise down the 2-1/2" x 12" tool support. Measure and mark points on this line, 2-1/2" in from each end. With a compass and using these points as centers, strike a 2-1/2" radius across each end of the board. Cut along the radii with a jigsaw.

8. To make holes for the handles of your tools, first measure 2" and 6" in from one end of the tool support and 2" in from the other; mark these points at the centerline. Then, using the 1-1/2" spade bit, drill a 1-1/2" hole at each of these three points.

9. Use glue and two No. 8 x 1-1/2" deck screws to fasten the tool support to the center support at the cross-line created in Step 6. Predrill the holes through the center support, using a No. 8 pilot bit with its stop collar set at 1-1/2"; avoid the center hole in the tool support.

10. On the front face of the center support, position and glue the two box sides, 4-3/4" down from the top of the arc; their outer surfaces should be 5-1/4" apart. Use a No. 8 pilot bit to predrill four holes, two pairs set 3-1/2" apart, through the center support and into the edges of the box sides. Set the stop collar at 1-1/2", and fasten each side with two No. 8 x 1-1/2" deck screws.

11. Glue and fasten the nine 3/4" x 5-1/4" slats across the face and bottom of the box, using four 16-gauge x 1-1/4" finish brads in each slat. Space the slats as desired. (Leaving equal distances of 3/16" between the six slats on the face and 1/4" between the remaining three on the bottom is easiest.)

12. Sand the completed box lightly; cypress needs no additional finish.

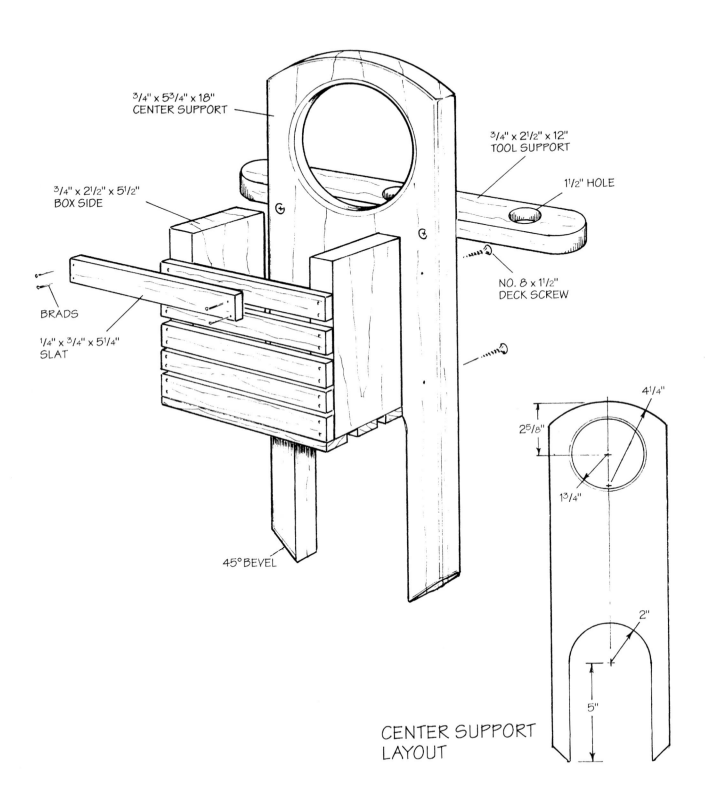

3/4" x 5 3/4" x 18"
CENTER SUPPORT

3/4" x 2 1/2" x 12"
TOOL SUPPORT

1 1/2" HOLE

3/4" x 2 1/2" x 5 1/2"
BOX SIDE

NO. 8 x 1 1/2"
DECK SCREW

BRADS

1/4" x 3/4" x 5 1/4"
SLAT

45° BEVEL

CENTER SUPPORT
LAYOUT

4 1/4"

2 5/8"

1 3/4"

2"

5"

PYRAMID PLANT STAND

THIS ELEGANT PROJECT DISPLAYS MORE GREENERY PER SQUARE FOOT OF SPACE THAN ALMOST ANY PLANT STAND YOU COULD BUY, AND UNLIKE ITS COMMERCIAL COUNTERPARTS, IT SHOULD LAST A LIFETIME. DURING WARM WEATHER, BRIGHTEN A PATIO OR DECK BY PLACING THE PYRAMID IN A SUNNY BUT SHELTERED SPOT. WHEN WINTER ARRIVES, MOVE THE PROJECT AND ITS LOVELY DISPLAY TO YOUR HOME'S INTERIOR.

Suggested Tools
Ripsaw
Crosscut saw
3/8" Drill
1/8" Drill bit
No. 8 Pilot bit and countersink with stop collar
Combination square
Router
1/4" Roundover bit
No. 2 Phillips screwdriver
36" Straightedge
Tape measure

Cut List
Cedar, redwood, or cypress is recommended for this project

1	Upright	1-1/2" x 1-1/2" x 40"
9	Octagons	3/4" x 7-1/4" x 7-1/4"
2	Upper arms	3/4" x 5-1/2" x 8"
4	Lower arms and legs	3/4" x 5-1/2" x 16-1/2"

Hardware and Supplies
No. 8 x 1-5/8" Deck screws
No. 8 x 2" Deck screw
No. 8 Finish washers
Tack glides (four)
Clear wood finish

Construction Procedure

1. To make the nine octagons from the 7-1/4" blanks, on each corner of all nine, measure 2-1/8" along both sides, and mark (see Octagon Layout). Use the straight edge of a combination square to strike a line between each set of points.

2. With a ripsaw, cut the corners from each square.

3. Use a 1/8" drill bit to bore a hole through the center of one octagon. Then strike a centerline across the middle of the remaining eight octagons. On each centerline, mark two points, 2-1/4" in from the edges of the octagon. Drill 1/8" holes at these points, using a No. 8 pilot bit to countersink the openings of each hole.

4. Use a 1/4" roundover bit in the router to round the top edges of the octagons.

5. Place each of the four 16-1/2" pieces lengthwise on a flat surface (see Leg and Lower Arm Layout), and make marks as follows: on the top edge, 1" and 4-1/2" over from the upper left corner; on the right edge, 3-1/2" down from the upper right corner—and 1" up from the lower right corner; on the left edge, 5" up from the lower left corner.

6. Use a straightedge to strike a diagonal line between the two 1" marks. Then use a combination square to strike lines perpendicular to the edges at the 4-1/2", 3-1/2", and 5" points. Cut each of the pieces on the diagonal line first. Then cut along the perpendicular lines to create the final shapes for the four legs and four lower arms.

7. To locate three screw-holes on each leg, measure 3/4" from the 5" end of the leg and 1-1/4" from the upper and lower edges, and mark. Then measure 1-7/8" in from the same end and 2-1/2" down from the upper edge, and mark.

8. On each lower arm piece, measure 3/4" from the 3-1/2" end and 3/4" from the upper and lower edges, and mark. Then measure 1-7/8" from the same end and 1-3/4" down from the upper edge, and mark.

9. Drill 1/8" holes through each of these marked points, 24 in all.

10. On each of the two 8" upper arm pieces, mark points 1" down (on one short end) from the upper left corner, and 1" up (on the other short end) from the lower right corner. Then mark points 2-5/8" up from the lower left corner, and 2-5/8" down from the upper right corner. With a straightedge, strike a diagonal line between the 1" points. Using a combination square, strike lines perpendicular to the edges at the 2-5/8" points.

11. Cut along the diagonal lines. Then cut along the perpendicular lines to shape the four upper arms.

12. To locate holes for the screws on each upper arm, measure 3/4" from the 2-5/8" end and 3/4" from the upper and lower edges, and mark. Then measure 1-7/8" in from the same end and 1-5/16" from the upper edge, and mark.

13. Drill 1/8" holes through each of the 12 marked points.

14. Fasten one leg flush to the bottom and side of the 40" upright and perpendicular to it, using No. 8 x 1-5/8" screws. Drive in only the two end screws to start, placing finish washers beneath their heads. Use the tip of the No. 8 pilot bit, stopped at 1-1/2", to cut the pilot holes in the upright.

15. Butt the next leg to the inside face of the first, and fasten it with two screws in a similar manner. Then use the third hole in the first leg to locate the pilot for the remaining screw, and fasten the third screw and washer set. Continue in this fashion until all four legs are attached. If you plan to situate the pyramid indoors, install tack glides on the lower edges of the legs.

16. Attach the lower arms in line with each of the four legs, with their short edges touching the legs and their long edges facing upward. Use the same method as before.

17. Measure 15-3/4" from the top of the upright, and use a square to carry a line around to each of the four sides. Fasten the four upper arms to the upright in the same manner as the lower arms; the long edges should be flush with the marked lines.

18. Mark a line on the upper edge of each lower arm, 5-3/4" from its outer end. Match the inside edge of an octagon to each line, and center the octagons over the arms. Fasten the four octagons with No. 8 x 1-5/8" deck screws, two screws per octagon, after predrilling the pilot holes with a No. 8 pilot bit.

19. Align the inside edge of each of the four upper octagons with the edge of the adjacent upper arm. Position all four octagons temporarily to assure that their shoulders meet symmetrically and that the mounting holes line up with the arms below. Fasten each one using a pair of No. 8 x 1-5/8" deck screws.

20. Center the uppermost octagon on the top of the upright, and fasten it with a No. 8 x 2" deck screw.

21. If the stand is to be left outdoors, apply two coats of clear wood finish.

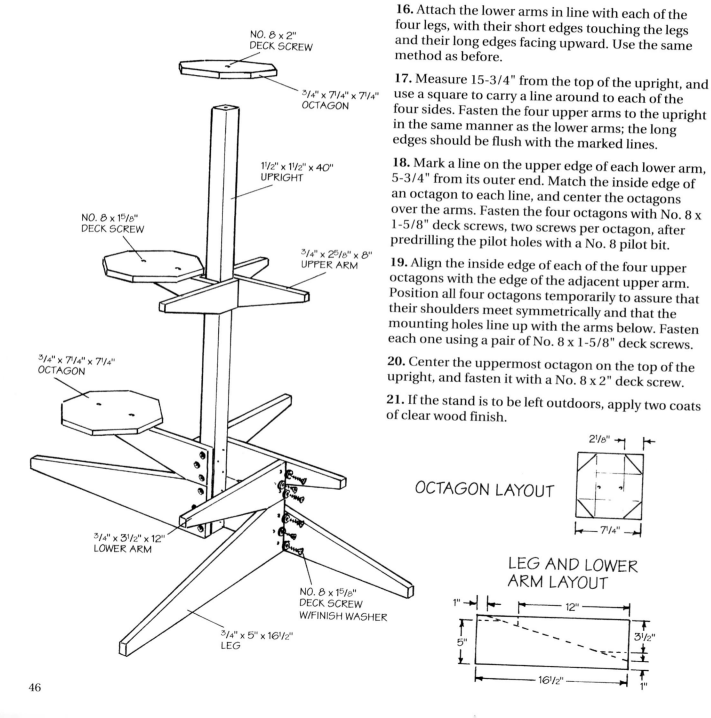

NO. 8 x 2" DECK SCREW

3/4" x 7¹/4" x 7¹/4" OCTAGON

1¹/2" x 1¹/2" x 40" UPRIGHT

NO. 8 x 1⁵/8" DECK SCREW

3/4" x 2⁵/8" x 8" UPPER ARM

3/4" x 7¹/4" x 7¹/4" OCTAGON

3/4" x 3¹/2" x 12" LOWER ARM

NO. 8 x 1⁵/8" DECK SCREW W/FINISH WASHER

3/4" x 5" x 16¹/2" LEG

OCTAGON LAYOUT

2¹/8"

7¹/4"

LEG AND LOWER ARM LAYOUT

1"

12"

5"

3¹/2"

16¹/2"

1"

HANDY BOX

TRUDGING BACK AND FORTH TO THE PLANTING BEDS
WHILE LADEN WITH TOOLS AND SUPPLIES CAN TURN
PLEASANT OUTDOOR TASKS INTO PURE DRUDGERY. TO
KEEP YOUR SPADES, HOES, CLIPPERS, TROWELS, GLOVES,
AND OTHER BACKYARD NECESSITIES RIGHT WHERE YOU
NEED THEM, CONSTRUCT THIS VERY HANDY BOX, AND
PLANT IT IN THE MIDDLE OF YOUR GARDEN.

Handy Box

Suggested Tools
    Table saw
    3/8" Drill
    No. 8 Pilot bit and countersink with stop collar
    3/32" Drill bit
    Router
    1/2" Straight bit
    Jigsaw
    Protractor
    24" Straightedge
    Tape measure
    Try square
    No. 2 Phillips screwdriver
    3/4" Chisel
    Tack hammer
    Nail set
    Palm sander
    Level
    Post-hole digger

Cut List
Cedar or redwood is recommended for this project.

2	Sides	3/4" x 11" x 11-3/8"
1	Floor	3/4" x 11-3/8" x 14-1/2"
1	Rear support	3/4" x 6-3/4" x 14-1/2"
1	Front support	3/4" x 1-1/4" x 14-1/2"
1	Front roof	3/4" x 4-3/8" x 19"
1	Rear roof	3/4" x 11-1/4" x 19"
2	Doors	3/4" x 7-7/8" x 8"
1	Base mount	3/4" x 1-1/2" x 12"
2	Post mounts	3/4" x 3" x 12"
1	Post	1-1/2" x 1-1/2" x 72"

Hardware and Supplies
    Waterproof wood glue
    No. 8 x 1-1/2" Deck screws
    16-gauge x 1-1/4" Finish brads
    1-1/2" x 1-1/2" Butt hinges (two sets)
    1-1/2" Hook and eye
    3" Utility hooks (three)
    5" Utility hook
    Exterior clear wood finish (optional)

Construction Procedure
1. To prepare each 11" x 11-3/8" side piece (see Side Layout), first mark the piece for cutting as follows: Measure up 7-1/4" from the 11-3/8" edge, and mark on the 11" edge. Then measure 9-3/16" up from the same 11-3/8" edge, and mark on the opposite 11" edge. From the first mark, draw a diagonal line up to the opposite corner. Then mark this diagonal line at 9-3/4", and draw a line from that point down to the 9-3/16" point marked earlier. By the protractor, the angle created for the roof peak should be 45°. Use a jigsaw to cut along the lines. Each finished side piece should measure 10-1/4" (from the peak to the bottom) x 11-3/8".

2. Set the table-saw blade at an 18° angle, and bevel one edge of the 6-3/4" x 14-1/2" rear support so that its finished width on its widest face remains at 6-3/4".

3. Reset the blade at a 27° angle, and bevel one edge of the 1-1/4" x 14-1/2" front support so that its finished width on one face remains at 1-1/4".

4. Set the blade at a 22-1/2° angle, and bevel both edges of each roof piece so that the angles are in opposite directions. The finished widths on the widest faces should be 4-3/8" and 11-1/4" respectively.

5. Butt the sides to the edges of the floor, and fasten each one with glue and three No. 8 x 1-1/2" deck screws, spaced 4-1/2" apart. Predrill the holes with the No. 8 pilot bit, setting the stop collar at 1-1/2".

6. Slip the rear support between the sides so that its beveled edge is flush with the rear slopes of the sides. Fasten with glue and three No. 8 x 1-1/2" deck screws, spaced 3" apart, on each side.

7. Slip the front support between the sides, and match the bevel to the front slope as before. Glue, and place one No. 8 x 1-1/2" deck screw through each corner. When drilling, set the stop collar at 1-1/2". Sand the entire project.

8. Temporarily position the doors with their 8" lengths running vertically, and mark positions for the 1-1/2" hinge sets, centering the hinges 5" apart on the edge of each side. Use the 1/2" straight bit in the router to mortise these locations to a depth of 1/8" for the hinges. Predrill the hinge holes with a 3/32" bit, and fasten the hinge leaves using the hardware provided with the hinge sets.

9. Mark the final positions of the doors, and fasten the hinges to them with the hardware provided. Install the hook-and-eye latch in the center of the doors, predrilling the holes with a 3/32" bit.

10. Fasten the roof pieces to the sides and supports with glue and 16-gauge x 1-1/4" finish brads. Space the brads 3" apart.

11. Center the 1-1/2" x 12" base mount over one end of the post. Check for square, glue, and fasten with one No. 8 x 1-1/2" deck screw. Then center the two 3" x 12" post mounts against the edges of the base mount so that their upper edges are flush with the top of the mount; fasten them with glue and two No. 8 x 1-1/2" deck screws through the post on each side, as well as four No. 8 x 1-1/2" deck screws, spaced 3" apart, placed along each edge. Predrill all holes with a No. 8 pilot bit, and set the stop collar at 1-1/2".

12. Turn the box over, and measure and mark a centerline down the length of the floor. Measure in 2" from each end along this line, and mark. Center the base mount between these two end marks, and use a No. 8 pilot bit to predrill four holes through the base and into the floor. Space the holes 3" apart, and set the stop collar at 1-1/4". Fasten the screws but do not countersink them fully or the points may exit through the floor.

13. Use the No. 8 pilot bit to predrill two holes, to a depth of 1", in the bottom edge of each post mount,

about 1-1/2" in from each end. Insert the 5" utility hook and the three 3" utility hooks into these four predrilled holes. Finish sanding the roof, doors, and mount assembly.

14. Use a post-hole digger to excavate a hole at the project site. Sink the post, check it on two faces with a level, and backfill the dirt.

15. If cedar or redwood is used, the project will need no finish, but several coats of an exterior clear wood finish will improve the appearance of the wood and help it to shed water.

 Tip

Screw depth is critical when the point of the screw is at risk of coming through a face board because of the way it's fastened. On the 3/4"-thick boards in this project, for example, the 1-1/2" screws driven through the 3/4" base mount could penetrate the 3/4" bottom of the box if they were countersunk too deeply. One solution is to stop the pilot hole at 1-1/4", and drive the screw so that its head is just above the surface of the wood. If the head must be set below the surface for the sake of appearance, just use a shorter (1-1/4") screw.

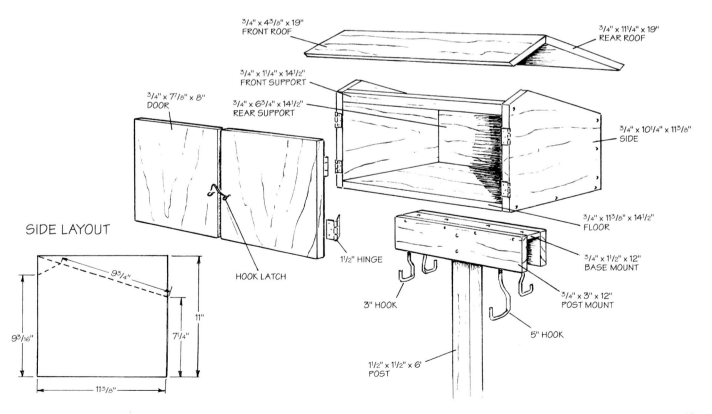

3/4" x 4³/₈" x 19" FRONT ROOF

3/4" x 11¹/₄" x 19" REAR ROOF

3/4" x 11¹/₄" x 14¹/₂" FRONT SUPPORT

3/4" x 7⁷/₈" x 8" DOOR

3/4" x 6³/₄" x 14¹/₂" REAR SUPPORT

3/4" x 10¹/₄" x 11³/₈" SIDE

SIDE LAYOUT

1¹/₂" HINGE

HOOK LATCH

3/4" x 11³/₈" x 14¹/₂" FLOOR

3/4" x 1¹/₂" x 12" BASE MOUNT

3/4" x 3" x 12" POST MOUNT

3" HOOK

5" HOOK

1¹/₂" x 1¹/₂" x 6' POST

9³/₄"

11"

7¹/₄"

9³/₁₆"

11³/₈"

TOOL SHELF

TRADITIONAL IN STYLE AND DEPENDABLE IN USE, THIS RACK HAS FOUR NOTCHES TO HOLD YOUR LARGEST GARDEN TOOLS AS WELL AS SHELF SPACE FOR THOSE EXTRAS LIKE GLOVES AND PLANTING CONTAINERS. FOR EVEN MORE STORAGE SPACE, SUSPEND SMALL TOOLS SUCH AS TROWELS AND CLIPPERS FROM HOOKS INSERTED INTO THE MOUNTING BOARD. EITHER ATTACH THE ASSEMBLED PROJECT TO AN INTERIOR WALL, OR CHOOSE AN OUTDOOR LOCATION THAT IS DRY AND WELL PROTECTED.

Suggested Tools

Table saw
3/8" Drill
No. 8 Pilot bit and countersink with stop collar
1-1/2" Spade bit
Jigsaw
Compass
Tape measure
Try square
No. 2 Phillips screwdriver
Palm sander

Cut List

Cypress is recommended for this project.

2	Rack and mounting board	3/4" x 6" x 60"
5	Rack support blanks	3/4" x 6" x 6"

Hardware and Supplies

Waterproof wood glue
No. 8 x 1-1/2" Deck screws
Exterior clear wood finish

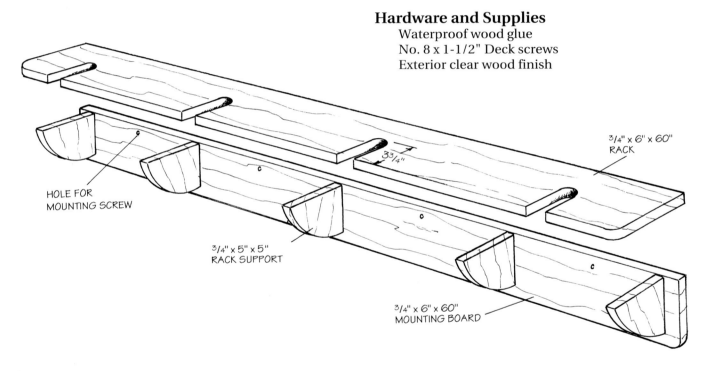

3/4" x 6" x 60" RACK

3 3/4"

HOLE FOR MOUNTING SCREW

3/4" x 5" x 5" RACK SUPPORT

3/4" x 6" x 60" MOUNTING BOARD

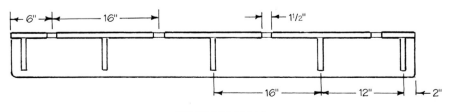

FRONT VIEW

Construction Procedure

1. On one of the 60" pieces, measure in 6" from each end, and use a square to mark across the board. Then strike lines across the board at 16" increments (see Front View). The four slots will be centered on these lines.

2. Using a square, mark parallel lines 3/4" to each side of the lines just marked.

3. From one long edge of this rack piece, measure in 3" and mark on each centerline. Drill through the board at each of these four intersection points, using a 1-1/2" spade bit. (Drill from both sides to avoid splintering the wood.)

4. With a jigsaw, cut along the parallel lines to the bore-hole points.

5. Next, you'll need to round the two outer corners of the rack. At each of the two corners on its long, cut edge, measure and mark a 2" square. Using the inside corner of each 2" square as a center, strike a 2" radius with a compass. Cut along the radius lines with a jigsaw. Repeat this procedure on the two opposite corners of the 60" mounting board. Sand both pieces.

6. Mount the slotted rack to the upper (uncut) face of the mounting board, flush with its edge; fasten it in place with glue and No. 8 x 1-1/2" deck screws, spaced 14" apart. Drill the holes with a No. 8 pilot bit, setting the stop collar at 1-1/2".

7. Cut five 3/4" x 6" x 6" blanks, as indicated in the Cut List. Strike a 5" radius on each piece, using a compass centered at one corner. Cut along the arcs with a jigsaw to complete the five rack supports. Sand them all well.

8. On the undersurface of the rack, measure and mark 2" in from each end (see Front View). Measure in 12" from each of these points, and mark again. To locate the center, measure in 16" from the marks just made, and mark once more.

9. Align each of the rack supports over the marked lines. True the pieces with a square. Use a No. 8 pilot bit, with the collar set at 1-1/2", to drill mounting holes into each edge of the rack supports, one through the rack and one through the mounting board. Fasten the supports with No. 8 x 1-1/2" deck screws and glue.

10. Finish the project with an exterior clear wood finish.

SQUIRREL WHIRLER

YES, IT WHIRLS SQUIRRELS, AND NO, THEY DON'T SEEM TO MIND. IN FACT, THE SQUIRRELS FAMILIAR WITH OUR FEEDER OBVIOUSLY LOVE IT. BUSHY-TAILED NEWCOMERS ARE A LITTLE SURPRISED THE FIRST TIME AROUND, WHEN THEY DISCOVER THAT THE EDIBLE TREAT DOESN'T COME WITHOUT A RIDE, BUT BEFORE LONG, THEY'LL HOP RIGHT ON EVEN WHEN WE'VE FORGOTTEN TO REPLACE THE EAR OF CORN.

Suggested Tools

Ripsaw
Crosscut saw
3/8" Drill
1/8", 11/64", 7/32", and 1/4" Drill bits
No. 8 Pilot bit and countersink with stop collar
Spokeshave (or router and 1/4" roundover bit)
No. 2 Phillips screwdriver
36" Straightedge
Tape measure
Protractor
Adjustable wrench

Cut List

Cedar, redwood, or cypress is recommended for this project.

1	Vertical mount	3/4" x 1-1/2" x 12"
1	Horizontal support	1-1/2" x 1-1/2" x 10"
1	Brace	3/4" x 7-1/4" x 7-1/4"
1	Paddle	3/4" x 7-1/4" x 48"
1	Retainer	3/4" x 3/4" x 3"

Hardware and Supplies

Waterproof wood glue
No. 8 x 1-1/4" Deck screws
No. 8 x 1-5/8" Deck screws
No. 8 x 2" Deck screws
1/4" x 3" Lag screw
1/4" Flat washers (two)
16d Galvanized ring shank nail
Clear wood finish

Construction Procedure

1. Using the No. 8 pilot bit with the stop collar set at 3/4", drill two holes, centered 1-1/2" apart, through the 3" retainer.

2. Drill two 7/32" mounting holes, 3/4" in from each end of the 12" vertical mount. Then set the stop collar on the No. 8 pilot bit at 3/4", and use it to drill three holes at points 3", 5", and 9" from one end of the mount.

3. Drill an 11/64" hole, 2" deep, into the center of one end of the 10" horizontal support. Then drill two 1/8" holes through one side, the first 1-1/2" from the undrilled end and the second 5" from the same end. Use the No. 8 pilot bit to countersink the openings of both 1/8" holes.

4. To form the brace, first measure 1" up from one corner of the 7-1/4" x 7-1/4" board. Then measure 1" over from the diagonally opposite corner. Use a straightedge to strike a line between these two points, and cut along the line with a crosscut saw.

5. Center the undrilled end of the horizontal support over the hole in the vertical mount that is 3" from the end of the mount. Use a No. 8 deck screw to mark a point on the support.

6. Place the brace over the remaining two holes on the vertical mount, and mark it in a similar manner.

7. Use the end of the No. 8 pilot bit to predrill the three marked holes to a depth of 3/4".

8. Spread glue along the line created by the three center holes in the vertical mount. Fasten the brace to the mount with two No. 8 x 1-5/8" deck screws. Then apply glue to the upper edge of the brace, and attach the horizontal support to the mount with another screw of the same size. Be sure that the two countersunk holes in the mount are facing upward.

9. Align the brace with the center of the horizontal support. With the No. 8 pilot bit, drill a pair of 1/2"-deep holes into the top of the brace. Do this by setting the stop collar at 2" and inserting the bit through the predrilled holes in the support.

10. Fasten the support to the brace with two No. 8 x 2" deck screws.

11. Mark a point 1-1/8" from one corner on the end of the 48" board; do the same at the diagonally opposite corner (see the smaller illustration). Strike a line between the two marks, using a straight board or a scrap of wood at least 4' in length. With a ripsaw, cut along the line; then choose the best piece to be your paddle.

12. Find and mark the center of the wide end of the paddle. Then use a protractor to locate points 22-1/2° from the straight edge, and mark them along

the sides of the board. Strike a line between the centerpoint and these two points, and cut along the lines.

13. Use a spokeshave to round the edges of both sides of the paddle. If you have access to a router, a 1/4" roundover bit can be used for this purpose.

14. Find the center of the narrow end of the paddle, and strike a centerline between it and the centerpoint at the opposite end. Mark a point along this line, 1-1/2" from the narrow end, and drill an 11/64" hole through the board. Then mark a point along the line, 26-7/8" from the wide end of the paddle, and drill a 1/4" hole.

15. Place a galvanized 16d ring shank nail into the hole at the narrow end of the paddle, and hold it in

place with the 3" retainer; secure the retainer with two No. 8 x 1-1/4" deck screws.

16. Fasten the paddle to the horizontal support with a 1/4" x 3" lag screw. Place a flat washer between the support and the paddle and another between the paddle and the head of the screw. Don't over-tighten the lag screw; the paddle should be free to rotate.

17. Sand the wood lightly, and apply two coats of clear wood finish.

18. Mount the whirler on a wall, post, or other vertical surface. Push an ear of dried corn over the exposed point of the nail; the rings on the nail will allow the ear to rotate.

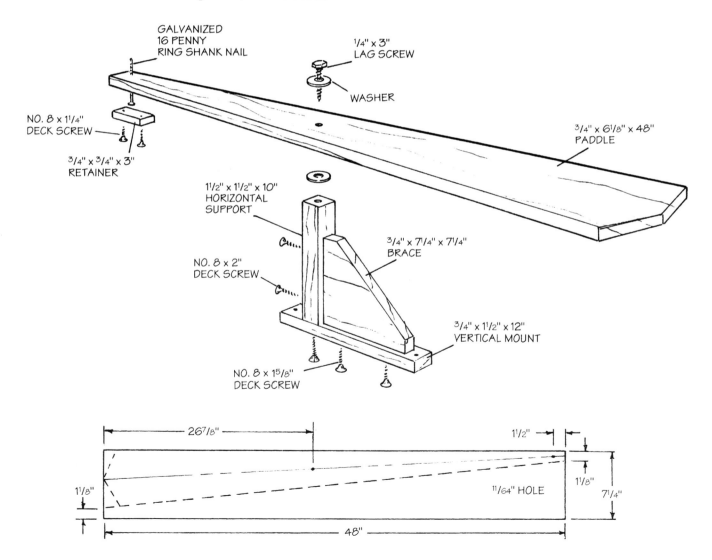

PICNIC TABLE FOR TWO

❧

THOUGH THIS PROJECT MAY NOT FEATURE
PROMINENTLY IN YOUR ANNUAL FAMILY REUNIONS,
IT'S PERFECT FOR THOSE SPECIAL DINING
EXPERIENCES—THE ONES YOU'D RATHER SHARE
WITH ONE SPECIAL PERSON. THE TABLE IS JUST
LARGE ENOUGH TO HOLD TWO PLACE SETTINGS.

PICNIC TABLE FOR TWO

Suggested Tools

Table saw
3/8" Drill
No. 8 and No 10 Pilot bits and countersinks
  with stop collars
1/4" Drill bit
Router
3/8" Roundover bit
Jigsaw
Compass
24" Straightedge
Tape measure
Try square
C-clamps
No. 2 Phillips screwdriver
Palm sander

Cut List

Cedar, redwood, or pressure-treated lumber is recommended for this project.

4	Main rails	3/4" x 3-1/2" x 60"
2	Uprights	3/4" x 3-1/2" x 16"
4	Table supports	3/4" x 3-1/2" x 28-1/2"
2	Table cross supports	3/4" x 3-1/2" x 30-1/2"
2	Braces	3/4" x 3-1/2" x 8"
1	Center support	3/4" x 3-1/2" x 25-1/2"
2	Top supports	1-1/2" x 3-1/2" x 27"
4	Table top	1-1/2" x 7-1/4" x 36"
2	Seats	1-1/2" x 8-1/2" x 16"

Hardware and Supplies

Waterproof wood glue
No. 8 x 1-1/2" Deck screws
No. 10 x 2-1/2" Deck screws
1/4" x 2-1/2" Carriage bolts with nuts (ten)
1/4" Flat washers (ten)
Exterior clear wood finish (optional)

Construction Procedure

1. Clamp two 60" main rails together, and drill two 1/4" holes, each 1-3/4" from an end and centered on the board. Repeat this process on the remaining two main rails.

2. Drill a 1/4" hole, 1-11/16" from one end and centered in each 16" upright. Drill another 1/4" hole, 4-3/4" from the opposite end of each board, centered as well.

3. Place the main rails on either side of the uprights, over the holes, so that two rails are flush to the top edge of the uprights and two are raised above the bottom edges of the uprights. Glue and fasten the joints with 1/4" x 2-1/2" carriage bolts and flat washers. Use the try square to make sure that the uprights are perpendicular to the rails.

4. Measure between the inside edges of the uprights to locate the centers of the upper and lower rail assemblies. Then measure 2-1/8" to one side of each center mark, and drill a 1/4" hole through both assemblies, centered at the widths of the boards.

5. Slip the 25-1/2" center support between the two main rail assemblies so that it's in line with the holes you just drilled. Use a square to assure that it's perpendicular to the rails. Then drill through the support with a 1/4" bit, using the holes in the upper and lower rails as guides. Fasten the support with glue and 1/4" x 2-1/2" carriage bolts and flat washers.

6. Clamp two 28-1/2" table supports together. Drill a 1/4" hole, 1-3/4" from one end and centered, and another 8-1/4" from the opposite end, also centered. Clamp the remaining two table supports together, and repeat this process.

7. Locate the center of the two 30-1/2" table cross supports, and mark a line with a square. Place one cross support on top of the lower rail assembly and against the center support, at the mark. Fasten the cross support in place with glue and two No. 8 x 1-1/2" deck screws, checking to see that it's square to the center support and main rails. Place the other cross support at the top of the center support, making sure that its edge is flush with the top edge of the support. Check and fasten it in the same manner.

8. Place one pair of 28-1/2" table supports at each end of the 30-1/2" table cross supports so that the edges of all the joints are flush. Clamp the outer boards in place, and run the 1/4" drill bit through the holes already drilled in the table supports. Fasten the four joints with glue and 1/4" x 2-1/2" carriage bolts and flat washers.

9. Set the table saw's miter gauge at a 45° angle. Trim the ends of the 8" braces to this angle so that the longest sides remain at 8". Place the braces between the lower cross support and the top edges of the lower rail, as shown in the illustration. Fasten them with glue and two No. 8 x 1-1/2" deck screws at each end.

10. Along one edge of each 27" top support, measure 12" in from each end, and mark. Measure 1-1/4" down from the corners on the opposite edge, and mark. Use a straightedge to draw a line between the 12" points and the 1-1/4" points on each piece. Cut along the lines with a jigsaw.

11. Locate the center of each top support, and mark a line at that point with a square. Measure 1-1/8" to each side of the line on both pieces, and make two more lines. Place the top supports at the upper outside edge of the table supports so that their uppermost edges are flush with the top surface of the table supports and the guidelines are visible. Fasten each top support with glue and two No. 10 x 2-1/2" deck screws.

12. Place the four 7-1/4" x 36" top boards onto the supports so that 2" of each board extends past the supports on each side. Space the boards 3/16" apart. Use a No. 8 pilot bit and countersink to drill through the top boards and into the supports beneath. Drill two holes, 5" apart, at each board end, and set the stop collar at 1-1/2". Lift each board to apply glue; then fasten it permanently with No. 8 x 1-1/2" deck screws.

13. Measure 2-1/2" in from the two edges of each corner, and mark. Strike a 2-1/2" radius from each of these four points with a compass. Then use a jigsaw to trim along the curved lines.

14. Locate the center of each 8-1/2" x 16" seat, and using a square, mark a line across the bottom surface. Mark lines 1-1/8" to either side of the center marks. Use these guidelines to position the seats onto the ends of the upper main rail. Glue and secure the seats with No. 10 x 2-1/2" deck screws fastened in a staggered pattern. You can predrill the holes using a No. 10 pilot bit, with the stop collar set at 2-1/2".

15. Using the method described in Step 13, mark, strike, and cut 2-1/2" radii at each corner of the two seats.

16. Using a 3/8" roundover bit in the router, round the top edges of the table and two seats.

17. Sand the surfaces of the table, the seats, and the upper main rail assembly. The completed table requires no finish if you use the recommended wood, but an exterior clear wood finish will help the table to shed water.

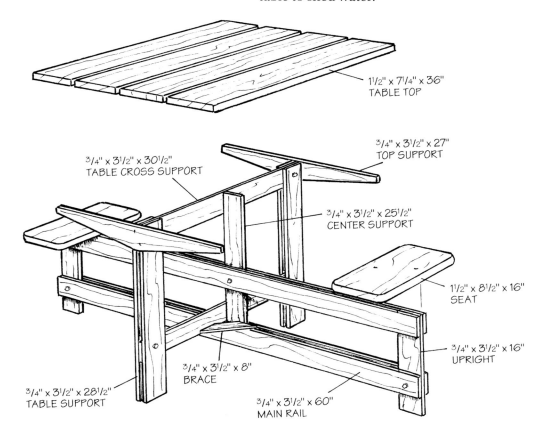

1½" x 7¼" x 36" TABLE TOP

¾" x 3½" x 27" TOP SUPPORT

¾" x 3½" x 30½" TABLE CROSS SUPPORT

¾" x 3½" x 25½" CENTER SUPPORT

1½" x 8½" x 16" SEAT

¾" x 3½" x 16" UPRIGHT

¾" x 3½" x 8" BRACE

¾" x 3½" x 28½" TABLE SUPPORT

¾" x 3½" x 60" MAIN RAIL

Cypress Doormat

A GOOD DOORMAT DOES TWO JOBS: IT KEEPS YOUR GAR-
DEN OUT OF YOUR HOUSE, AND IT LOOKS ATTRACTIVE
FOR MORE THAN A DAY OR TWO. UNLIKE THE HEMP AND
RUBBER MODELS, THIS SLATTED, CYPRESS MAT WON'T
SHED OR GET SOGGY. WHAT'S MORE, THE DIRT THAT IT
COLLECTS WON'T STICK RIGHT BACK TO YOUR SHOES—IT
FALLS STRAIGHT THROUGH THE CYPRESS SLATS INSTEAD.

Suggested Tools

Table saw
3/8" Drill
No. 6 Pilot bit and countersink with stop collar
24" Straightedge
Tape measure
Framing square
Pipe clamps
Tack hammer
Nail set
No. 2 Phillips screwdriver
Palm sander

Cut List

Cypress is recommended for this project.
10 Long slats   3/4" x 3/4" x 30"
18 Short slats   3/4" x 3/4" x 5-1/2"
 2 End slats   3/4" x 3/4" x 14-1/4"

Hardware and Supplies

Waterproof wood glue
No. 6 x 1-1/4" Deck screws
16-gauge x 1-1/4" Finish brads

Construction Procedure

1. Glue one 5-1/2" short slat to each end of a 30" long slat, making sure that all the ends are flush. Fasten the short slats using two 16-gauge x 1-1/4" finish brads on each piece.

2. Fasten another long slat to the short slats just nailed, using the same technique. Follow with two more short slats at the ends, and repeat the process until the final long slat is attached. Use a straight-edge and square as you work to ensure that the pieces remain flush and square.

3. Hold the assembly together with a pair of clamps, taking care not to over-tighten them, while the glue sets and dries overnight. Use a wet cloth to wipe any excess glue from the joints before the glue hardens.

4. Place the two 14-1/4" end slats over the ends; fasten them with glue and one No. 6 x 1-1/4" deck screw at each corner. Predrill the holes with a No. 6 pilot bit, and set the stop collar at 1-1/4" so that the screw heads will be flush with the surface of the wood.

5. If cypress is used, no finish is required.

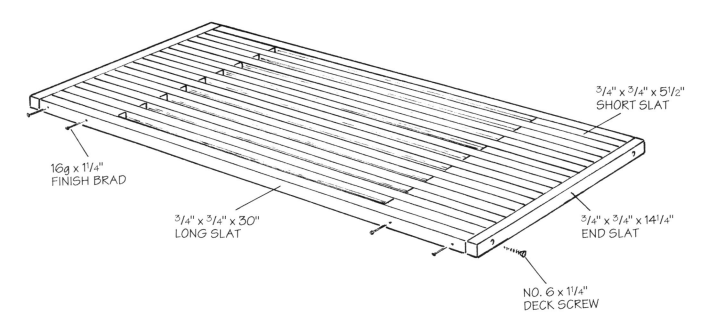

3/4" x 3/4" x 5 1/2"
SHORT SLAT

16g x 1 1/4"
FINISH BRAD

3/4" x 3/4" x 30"
LONG SLAT

3/4" x 3/4" x 14 1/4"
END SLAT

NO. 6 x 1 1/4"
DECK SCREW

CROSSING SIGNS

IF YOU CAN'T BEAT 'EM, JOIN 'EM. INSTEAD OF
LETTING GARDEN PESTS DRIVE YOU CRAZY EACH
YEAR, WHY NOT GIVE IN WITH GOOD GRACE—
AND A SENSE OF HUMOR? WELCOME AND DIRECT
ANIMAL VISITORS WITH CROSSING SIGNS, ONES
BOUND TO KEEP YOUR FAMILY ENTERTAINED
EVEN IF THEY DON'T PREVENT JAYWALKING.

Suggested Tools

3/8" Drill
No. 6 Pilot bit and countersink with stop collar
Jigsaw
Compass
36" Straightedge
Try square
No. 2 Phillips screwdriver
Palm sander

Cut List

Cedar is recommended for this project.

3 Animal blanks 3/4" x 8" x 11"
3 Backers   3/4" x 11-1/4" x 11-1/4"
3 Stakes   3/4" x 1-3/4" x 20-1/2"

Hardware and Supplies

Waterproof wood glue
No. 6 x 1-1/4" Deck screws
Exterior latex paint

Construction Procedure

1. The easiest way to transfer the animal patterns is to make three copies of the grid pattern provided, trace the animal patterns (also provided) onto the grids, and then enlarge the grids by 275%.

2. Cut out each paper-animal silhouette, and trace its outline onto the three 8" x 11" blanks. Then use a jigsaw with a fine-toothed blade to cut the boards to shape. Sand the faces and edges, and paint the shapes in the color of your choice, using an exterior latex.

3. With a compass, strike an 11-1/4"-diameter circle on the face of each 11-1/4"-square backer. Cut the three circles with a jigsaw, and then sand their edges.

4. Center and glue the animal cutouts onto the circular backers. Use the No. 6 pilot bit, with the stop collar set at 1-1/4", to predrill two screw holes through each backer and into its cutout; locate these holes to enter substantial parts of the animal cutouts, but avoid the centers, where stakes will be mounted. Drive in two No. 6 x 1-1/4" screws.

5. Trim one end of each stake to make a sharp point. Position a stake on the rear of each backer so that it's centered and the animal is level. Predrill two holes about 8" apart into the stake and backer, using the No. 6 pilot bit with the stop set at 1-1/4". Fasten the stakes with No. 6 x 1-1/4" screws.

6. If cedar is used, no finish is required.

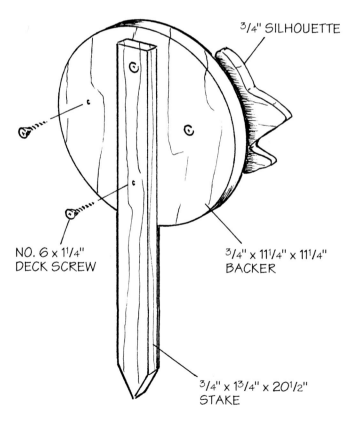

3/4" SILHOUETTE

NO. 6 x 1¹/4"
DECK SCREW

3/4" x 11¹/4" x 11¹/4"
BACKER

3/4" x 1³/4" x 20¹/2"
STAKE

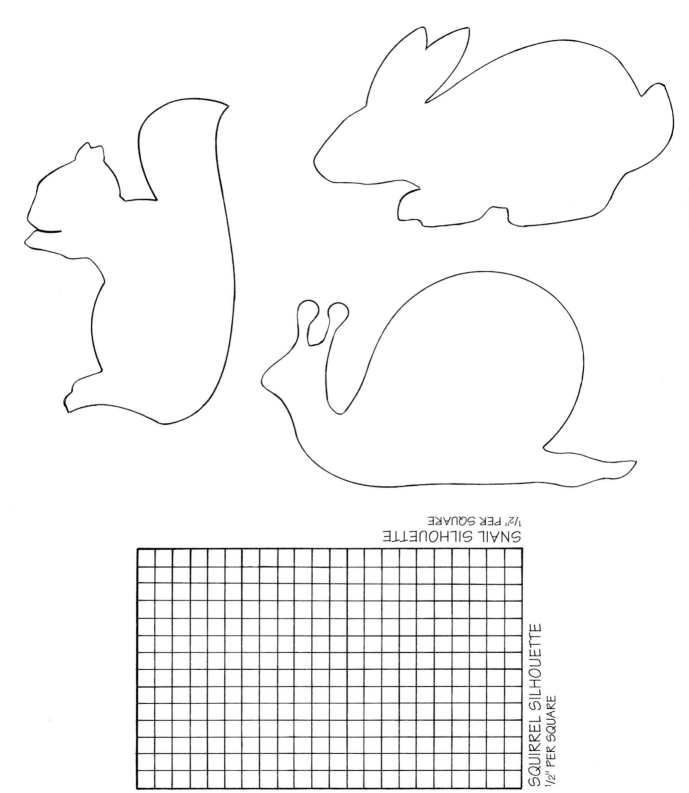

SNAIL SILHOUETTE
1/2" PER SQUARE

SQUIRREL SILHOUETTE
1/2" PER SQUARE

RABBIT SILHOUETTE
1/2" PER SQUARE

BIRD FEEDER

❧

WHAT WOULD A GARDEN BE WITHOUT A BIRD FEEDER? MUCH LESS ENTERTAINING. THE PROJECT PRESENTED HERE IS BASED ON A CLASSIC, FLY-THROUGH DESIGN, BUT ITS CLEAR ACRYLIC ROOF EXPANDS YOUR VIEWING AREA CONSIDERABLY. THE WIRE-MESH BOTTOM IS EASY TO CLEAN, AND THE OVERALL DESIGN IS SO ATTRACTIVE THAT YOU MAY END UP GAZING AT THE FEEDER EVEN WHEN THERE AREN'T ANY BIRDS GAZING BACK.

BIRD FEEDER

Suggested Tools

Crosscut saw
3/8" Drill
1/8", 3/16", and 1/4" Drill bits
No. 6 Pilot bit and countersink with stop collar
Router
1/4" Roundover bit
No. 2 Phillips screwdriver
Combination square
Staple gun
Tack hammer
Nail set
36" Straightedge

Cut List

Cedar, redwood, or cypress is recommended for this project.

1	Uprights	3/4" x 5-1/2" x 24"
1	Center support	1-1/2" x 1-1/2" x 13"
1	Corner mold	3/4" x 18" corner molding
1	Tray sides and fronts	3/4" x 1-1/2" x 48"
1	Screen retainers	3/4" x 3/4" x 48"

Hardware and Supplies

1/8" x 7-1/2" x 18" Clear acrylic panels with buffed edges (two)
6-gauge x 1-3/8" Screw eyes (two)
No. 6 x 1-1/4" Deck screws
No. 6 Finish washers (four)
16-gauge x 1-1/4" Finish brads
1/8" x 36" Nylon cord
9-1/2" x 16" Aluminum window screen
5/16" Staples

Construction Procedure

1. To make the tray fronts and sides, cut the 3/4" x 1-1/2" x 48" piece into two 16" lengths and two 8" lengths. On the longer pieces, center and mark points 3/8" in from each end. On the shorter lengths, center and mark points 2-1/4" in from each end.

2. Use a No. 6 pilot bit and countersink to drill holes at these points. Set the stop collar so that the screw heads will be flush with the surface of the wood.

3. To make the screen retainer pieces, cut the 3/4" x 3/4" x 48" piece into two 16" lengths and two 8"

lengths. On each of the longer pieces, locate and mark the center. Then mark points 6" to either side of the center. On the shorter pieces, measure and mark points 2" in from each end.

4. Use the No. 6 pilot bit and countersink to drill holes at these points. Set the countersink depth as before.

5. Assemble the rectangular tray by fastening the 16" tray fronts to the ends of the two 8" tray sides with No. 6 x 1-1/4" deck screws. All outside edges should be flush.

6. With 5/16" staples, fasten the aluminum window screen to the bottom of the tray.

7. Attach the screen retainer strips to the tray, with the screen in between. Use No. 6 x 1-1/4" deck screws in the holes drilled earlier. Rout the upper edges of the frame with a 1/4" roundover bit if desired.

8. To make the uprights, first cut two 10-1/2" lengths from the 24" piece of wood. Measure and strike a line down the center of each piece. Then, on one end of each piece, use a combination square to strike 45° lines from the centerpoint to both sides. Cut on the marked lines.

9. Use a No. 6 pilot bit and countersink to drill two holes through each upright, 7/8" and 1-3/8" down from the pointed end and located on the centerline. Set the stop collar to countersink the upper holes for screw heads.

10. Place the screened tray flat, with the screen towards the bottom. Center the uprights against the insides of the tray sides. To attach the uprights, drive a pair of No. 6 x 1-1/4" deck screws through the two predrilled holes in each tray side.

11. Place the 13" center support between the uprights, with one corner facing upward and two sides flush with the upper edges of the uprights. Secure the support with two No. 6 x 1-1/4" deck screws in the upper holes in the uprights and two 1-3/8" screw eyes in the lower holes.

12. Place the clear acrylic panels over the uprights so that their uppermost edges meet at the peak of the center support. Measure down 2-3/4" from this joint along the center of each 45° edge on both uprights, and mark the panels. Then lay them on a piece of scrap wood, and drill 3/16" holes at the four marked points.

13. Use a 1/8" drill bit to make pilot holes in the edges of the uprights, at the points where the panels will be fastened to the wood. Then carefully attach the panels to the uprights, using four No. 6 x 1-1/4" deck screws and finish washers. Do not over-tighten; the plastic will crack if you do.

14. Center the 18" corner molding over the plastic roof peak, and drill three 1/8" holes, evenly spaced, through the molding and the plastic beneath. Secure the cap with 16-gauge x 1-1/4" brads. Use a nail set to seat the heads.

15. Carefully drill 1/4" holes through the corner mold, directly over each screw eye. Thread the 1/8" nylon cord through the holes, and tie each end to the eyes.

16. This project will weather outdoors; no finish is needed.

 Tips

Clear acrylic plastic sheeting is durable once it's in place, but working with it can be difficult. To saw acrylic, use a fine-toothed blade when possible. On a 10" table saw, use a blade that has 40 or more teeth per inch; reciprocating jigsaw blades should have blades of 10 or 12 teeth per inch. Place masking tape over the cut site, mark your cutting line, and remove the tape once the cut has been made.

Drilling acrylic sheet requires a sharp bit. Back the plastic with scrap wood so that the bit will bury itself in the wood.

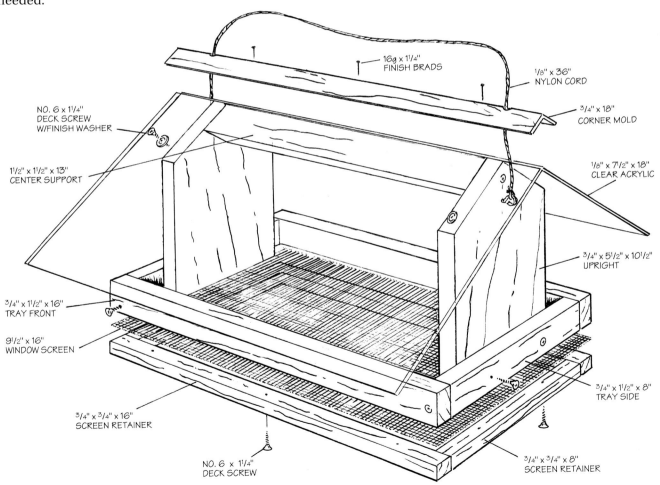

16g x 1¼"
FINISH BRADS

1/8" x 36"
NYLON CORD

NO. 6 x 1¼"
DECK SCREW
W/FINISH WASHER

¾" x 18"
CORNER MOLD

1½" x 1½" x 13"
CENTER SUPPORT

1/8" x 7½" x 18"
CLEAR ACRYLIC

¾" x 5½" x 10½"
UPRIGHT

¾" x 1½" x 16"
TRAY FRONT

9½" x 16"
WINDOW SCREEN

¾" x 1½" x 8"
TRAY SIDE

¾" x ¾" x 16"
SCREEN RETAINER

NO. 6 x 1¼"
DECK SCREW

¾" x ¾" x 8"
SCREEN RETAINER

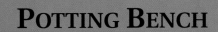

POTTING BENCH

THIS ELEGANT POTTING BENCH PROVIDES PLENTY OF SPACE FOR WORK AND STORAGE, BUT IT'S SMALL ENOUGH TO FIT TIDILY INTO ANY CORNER OF YOUR SHED OR GARAGE. WHAT'S MORE, IT'S A PROJECT THAT EVEN A BEGINNER CAN PUT TOGETHER IN A DAY.

Suggested Tools

Table saw
3/8" Drill
No. 10 Pilot bit and countersink with stop collar
1/8" Drill bit with stop collar
3/16" Extension bit with stop collar
1/4" Drill bit
7-1/16" Drill bit with stop collar
Jigsaw
Tape measure
24" Straightedge
Try square
C-clamps
Protractor
No. 2 Phillips screwdriver
Hammer
Adjustable wrench
Tack hammer
Nail set
Palm sander

Cut List

Western red cedar is recommended for this project.

Qty	Part	Dimensions
1	Shelf	3/4" x 7-1/4" x 39"
1	Shelf back	3/4" x 7-1/4" x 39"
1	Detail	1-1/2" x 3-1/2" x 5-1/4"
2	Shelf support	3/4" x 6-1/4" x 10-1/4"
2	Standards	3/4" x 5-1/4" x 15"
1	Table back	3/4" x 9-1/4" x 39"
4	Table boards	1-1/2" x 5-1/4" x 39"
1	Front apron	1-1/2" x 3-1/2" x 36"
2	Side aprons	1-1/2" x 3-1/2" x 20"
2	Braces	1-1/2" x 3-1/2" x 15"
4	Legs	1-1/2" x 3-1/2" x 31-1/2"
1	Shelf back	3/4" x 5-1/4" x 33"
3	Shelf boards	1-1/2" x 5-1/4" x 30"
1	Shelf board	1-1/2" x 3-1/2" x 30"
2	Shelf supports	1-1/2" x 1-3/4" x 20"

Hardware and Supplies

Waterproof wood glue (optional)
No. 10 x 1-1/4" Deck screws
No. 10 x 2-1/2" Deck screws
6d Galvanized casing nails
1/4" x 3-1/2" Carriage bolts and nuts (twelve)
1/4" x 5-1/2" Carriage bolts and nuts (four)
1/4" Flat washers (sixteen)
Exterior clear wood finish

Construction Procedure

1. This project is easier to assemble if the screw and bolt holes are predrilled. Turn the front and side apron pieces on edge, and mark the following on a penciled centerline: On the side aprons, measure from one end, and mark at 2-1/4", 4", 7-3/4", 9-1/2", 13-3/4", 15", and 18-3/4". On the front apron, measure from one end, and mark at 1", 12", 24", and 35". Bore all the marked points with a 7/16" bit to a depth of 1-3/4", keeping the bit straight as you work. Then use a 3/16" bit to drill from those points through the wood.

2. Turn the bottom shelf supports on their 1-3/4" edge, and mark at these points, measured from one end, on a penciled centerline: 1", 5", 6-1/2", 10-1/2", 12", 16", and 19". With a 3/16" bit, bore all the marked points straight through on both pieces.

3. On the top shelf piece, mark points 4-1/4" from the ends and 1-1/8" from the edges. Drill through at these points, using a No. 10 pilot bit with the stop collar set at 1-3/8".

4. On the upper back piece, first locate the center of the board; then measure down 2" from the top edge at that point, and mark. Measure 17-3/8" in from each end, and mark on the upper edge. Then draw diagonal lines from those two points to the 2" mark. Cut along the lines to remove a V-shaped notch. To locate the holes, mark points 2-1/2" and 6" from the ends and 3/4" and 2-1/8" from one edge. Then measure and mark 4-1/4" from the opposite edge and 13" in from each end. Drill through as before.

5. Measure and mark each of the top shelf standards as follows: 1" and 6-3/8" from one end and 1" in from each side; and, on a lengthwise centerline, 7-3/4" and 12" from the same end. Again, use a No. 10 pilot bit stopped at 1-3/8" to bore through the wood.

6. The table back should first be marked to cut the corner notches. Use a square to draw a line 3-1/2" from one edge at the corners and 1-1/2" from the ends. Cut with a jigsaw. Then, to locate the holes, mark the board at points 4-1/2" from the same edge and 1", 9", and 16" from each end. Finally, place two more holes 1" from each end and 2-1/2" from the shoulders of the just-cut notches. Drill all holes with a No. 10 pilot bit stopped as before.

7. The bottom shelf back is first marked and cut to remove a V-shaped notch, as described in Step 4. Then mark for holes at points 1" in from the ends and edges at the corners. That done, mark for holes 7" and 14" in from the ends, 2-1/2" from the unnotched edge.

8. Mark each top shelf support as follows: First draw a diagonal line from the upper left corner to the

GARDEN GONG

WHETHER YOU'D LIKE TO ADD A TOUCH OF THE UNUSU-
AL TO AN OTHERWISE CLASSIC GARDEN OR SUMMON
YOUR CHILDREN FROM THE NEIGHBOR'S YARD, THIS DRA-
MATIC GONG WILL DO THE JOB. IT'S A RELATIVELY EASY
PROJECT TO CONSTRUCT, TOO; THE MOST DIFFICULT STEP
YOU'LL FACE IS DIGGING THE MOUNTING HOLE.

Suggested Tools

Table saw
3/8" Drill
No. 8 Pilot bit and countersink with stop collar
1/8" Extension bit
1/8" and 3/16" Drill bits
3/4" Forstner bit
Jigsaw
Coping saw
Compass
Tape measure
Try square
No. 2 Phillips screwdriver
Pliers
Level
Post-hole digger
Palm sander

Cut List

Cedar is recommended for this project.

1	Post	3-1/2" x 3-1/2" x 42"
2	Cross supports	1-1/2" x 5-1/4" x 23-1/2"
1	Vertical support	1-1/2" x 3-1/2" x 37"
1	Brace	3-1/2" x 3-1/2" x 12"

Hardware and Supplies

Waterproof wood glue
19" Steel platter
3/8" x 6" Decorative chains (two)
1" S-hooks (two)
1-5/8" Screw eyes (two)
2-5/8" Screw eyes (two)
3/4" x 22" Dowel
Wooden ball, 2"-diameter
No. 8 x 2" Deck screws
No. 8 x 3" Deck screws

Construction Procedure

1. To round the ends of the 23-1/2" cross supports, first locate and mark centerlines along the length of each one. Then measure 4" in from each end, and mark across the line. With a compass, and using the marked points as centers, mark a 4" radius across each end of both pieces. Cut along the curved lines with a jigsaw.

2. Position one of the cross supports at one end of the 42" post so that its upper edge is flush with the top of the post and one radius cut extends beyond the post. Check with a square to assure that the support is perpendicular, and then use a No. 8 pilot bit to drill three holes, 3" apart, in a triangular pattern, through the support and into the post behind. Set the stop collar at 2". Fasten the pieces with glue and No. 8 x 3" deck screws.

3. To locate the curved cut on the 12" brace, first measure 4-1/2" up from one end, and mark on the edge of the brace. Use a compass to draw a 1-1/2" radius from this point toward the center of the wood. With a square, continue the line from the arc down to the same end of the brace from which you first measured; this line will be 1-1/2" from the edge of the brace. Cut along the marked line with a coping saw.

4. Set the square end of the brace flush with the end of the post and cross support. The brace's curve should face in the same direction as the long extension of the cross support. Use a No. 8 pilot bit to drill three holes in line, 4" apart, through the brace and into the post. Standard bits are not long enough to accomplish this in one step, so you may have to use a 1/8" extension bit to complete the work. Set the stop collar at 2" for the hole in the lower part of the brace, and remove it entirely for the holes in the full part of the brace. You may have to use a 5/16" bit to bore a deeper head socket if your countersink bit is too short to penetrate at least 1" beyond the face of the brace. Fasten with glue and No. 8 x 3" deck screws.

5. With the No. 8 pilot bit, predrill two more holes, 3" apart, through the cross support and into the brace behind it; set the stop collar at 2". Fasten the pieces with two more No. 8 x 3" screws.

6. Position the 37" vertical support so that its bottom edge is flush with the lower edge of the mounted cross support and the radius-cut end of the cross support extends past the vertical support. Check for

PLANTER

Suggested Tools

 Table saw
 3/8" Drill
 No. 6 and 8 Pilot bits and countersinks
   with stop collars
 Jigsaw
 Tape measure
 Try square
 No. 2 Phillips screwdriver
 Tack hammer
 Nail set
 Pipe clamps
 Palm sander

Cut List

Cypress is recommended for this project.

8	Side panels	3/4" x 5" x 30"
2	Top rails	1-7/16" x 1-1/2" x 11-1/2"
2	Top rails	1-7/16" x 1-1/2" x 12-7/8"
2	Bottom supports	3/4" x 3/4" x 10"
2	Bottom supports	3/4" x 3/4" x 7"
1	Bottom	3/4" x 8-1/2" x 10"
4	Trim strips	3/4" x 3/4" x 28-1/2"

Hardware and Supplies

 Waterproof wood glue
 No. 6 x 1-1/4" Deck screws
 No. 8 x 1-1/2" Deck screws
 16-gauge x 1-1/4" Finish brads

Construction Procedure

1. Measure down 12" from one end of each of the eight 5" x 30" side panels, and mark on one edge. From this point, use a compass to scribe a 3-1/8" radius from edge to edge (see Side Panel Detail; note that this illustration shows two assembled side panels). Then measure in 5/8" from the same edge, and draw a line from the lower end of the arc to the bottom of the board. Use a jigsaw to cut along the straight line and the arc on each piece.

2. Next, you'll need to construct four corner assemblies by butting the four pairs of side panels together at right angles. As you do this, study the Planter illustration carefully. The eight side panels must be assembled exactly as shown; if the four corner assemblies are butted incorrectly, the dimensions of your planter will change. Fasten each pair of panels

with glue and No. 8 x 1-1/2" deck screws. Before inserting the screws, check the trueness of the angles with a square. Use a No. 8 pilot bit, stopped at 1-1/2", to predrill the holes 7" apart.

3. Measure down 8" from the top edge of each corner assembly, and mark a line across both inside surfaces. Glue and clamp two of the four corner assemblies together at the radius-cut edges to make an inside surface that is 10" in width, making sure that the upper and lower edges are flush. Glue and fasten one 10" bottom support just below the 8" line marked earlier, using four countersunk No. 6 x 1-1/4" deck screws, placed 2" apart. Repeat the process with the other two corner assemblies. Allow both sections to dry overnight.

4. Glue and clamp both halves together so that their edges match and the sections are flush top and bottom. Fasten the 7" bottom supports in line with the 10" supports already in place, using the method described in Step 3; space these screws 1-1/4" apart.

5. Mount each of the 11-1/2" top rails to the face of two butted side panels so that its top and the upper edge of the side panels are flush. The 1-1/2" faces should meet the side panels. Use a No. 8 pilot bit to counterbore the holes to a depth of 2"; then fasten with glue and two No. 8 x 1-1/2" deck screws, spaced about 5" apart.

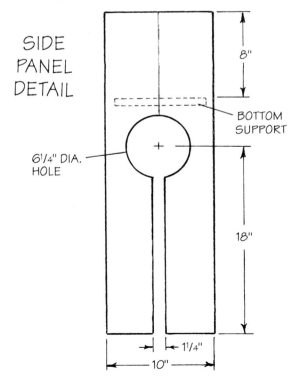

SIDE PANEL DETAIL

6 1/4" DIA. HOLE

8"

BOTTOM SUPPORT

18"

1 1/4"

10"

6. Mount each of the 12-7/8" top rails in the same manner. The ends of the rails should be flush with the sides of the two rails already in place.

7. Fasten the 8-1/2" x 10" bottom piece to the tops of the supports, using four No. 6 x 1-1/4" deck screws, one placed at each side.

8. Set the table saw to cut at a depth of 1/2". Then cut 1/2" x 1/2" dadoes into one face of each 28-1/2" trim strip. Do this by first setting the fence 1/2" from the blade. Then pass each strip through, turn it end-for-end and 1/4-turn clockwise, and pass it through again.

9. Mount the strips to the outside corners of the planter, using glue and 16-gauge x 1-1/4" finish

brads. Space the brads 6" apart, and set them below the surface of the wood.

10. Sand the trim and the outside of the planter. Cypress requires no finish.

 Tip

It's possible to avoid the tedious job of butt-joining the side panels to make individual corner assemblies. Just substitute four 1 x 12s for the eight 3/4" x 5" pieces recommended. Cut each piece to 10" in width, and draw a centerline down its length. Then follow the existing instructions to make the cutouts and side slots, and join the four sides together in traditional box fashion. Drive the screws for the bottom supports by reaching through the open cutouts.

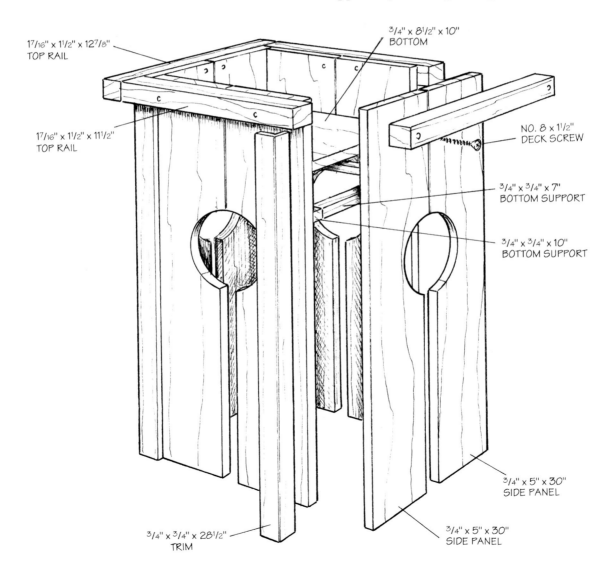

17/16" x 1 1/2" x 12 7/8"
TOP RAIL

3/4" x 8 1/2" x 10"
BOTTOM

17/16" x 1 1/2" x 11 1/2"
TOP RAIL

NO. 8 x 1 1/2"
DECK SCREW

3/4" x 3/4" x 7"
BOTTOM SUPPORT

3/4" x 3/4" x 10"
BOTTOM SUPPORT

3/4" x 5" x 30"
SIDE PANEL

3/4" x 3/4" x 28 1/2"
TRIM

3/4" x 5" x 30"
SIDE PANEL

STRAWBERRY PYRAMID

HANDSOME, EFFECTIVE, AND SPACE-SAVING, THIS THREE-PIECE PROJECT WILL MAKE A HEALTHY HOME FOR ALMOST ANY KIND OF SMALL VEGETABLE, THOUGH STRAWBERRIES ARE PARTICULARLY WELL-SUITED TO ITS LAYERED CONSTRUCTION. VIGOROUS RUNNERS WILL SPREAD AND DESCEND UNTIL THE WHOLE STRUCTURE IS COVERED WITH LUSH GROWTH. ARRANGE THE FRAMES AS SHOWN IN THE PHOTO, OR PLACE THEM (AS THE ILLUSTRATOR HAS) WITH THEIR SIDES RUNNING PARALLEL TO ONE ANOTHER.

Suggested Tools
   Table saw
   3/8" Drill
   No. 8 Pilot bit and countersink with stop collar
   Jigsaw
   Compass
   Tape measure
   Try square
   No. 2 Phillips screwdriver
   Palm sander

Cut List
Cedar is recommended for this project.

4	Frames	3/4" x 5-1/2" x 48"
4	Frames	3/4" x 5-1/2" x 32"
4	Frames	3/4" x 5-1/2" x 21"
12	Corner braces	1-1/2" x 1-1/2" x 4-1/4"

Hardware and Supplies
   No. 8 x 1-1/2" Deck screws

Construction Procedure
1. Trim the 5-1/2" frame pieces to 48", 32", and 21" in length, as indicated in the Cut List.

2. On each piece, measure 6" in from each end, and mark the edge of the board. Use these marks as centers to strike 1" radii (see Frame Detail).

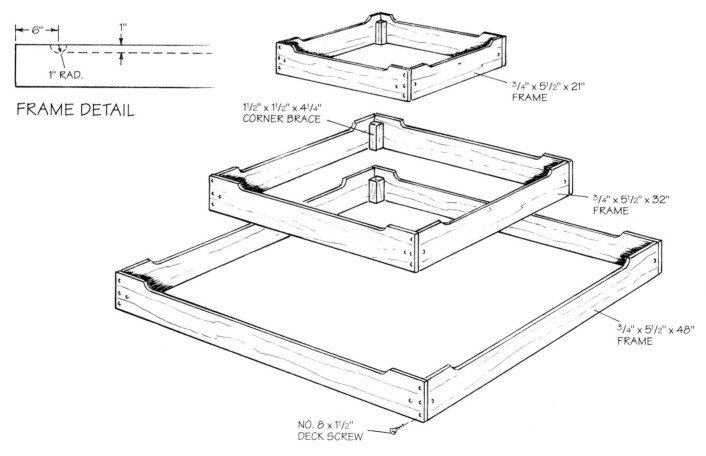

FRAME DETAIL

1 1/2" x 1 1/2" x 4 1/4" CORNER BRACE

3/4" x 5 1/2" x 21" FRAME

3/4" x 5 1/2" x 32" FRAME

3/4" x 5 1/2" x 48" FRAME

NO. 8 x 1 1/2" DECK SCREW

3. Measure in 1" from the marked edges, and strike a line to connect the two radii on each board.

4. With a jigsaw, cut along the line and the quarter-sectors marked at each radius.

5. Sand all the cut edges.

6. Butt two of the 48" frames to the ends of the other two 48" frames so that they form a 48" x 49-1/2" rectangle. Make sure that the 1"-radius reliefs all face upward.

7. Place one of the 4-1/4" braces inside each corner, flush with the unradiused (lower) edge of the frame. Using a No. 8 pilot bit and countersink, with the stop collar set at 1-1/2", drill two holes at each corner, one through each frame piece and into the brace; position these holes far enough apart so that the tips

of the screws don't meet inside the brace. Fasten the frames to the braces with eight No. 8 x 1-1/2" deck screws.

8. Drill a set of three pilot holes, 2" apart, through the frames at each corner and into the ends of the abutting frames (see the illustration).

9. Then fasten the corners of the frames with twelve No. 8 x 1-1/2" deck screws.

10. Repeat this assembly process with the 32" and the 21" frame pieces.

11. No finish is required with cedar. To assemble the pyramid, set the largest frame down first, and fill it with a mixture of topsoil and compost. Then position and fill the next largest frame. The smallest frame, which goes on top, must be filled last.

LIGHT BOX

FOR FULL ENJOYMENT OF YOUR BACKYARD OR GARDEN, OUTDOOR LIGHTING IS A MUST. THIS DECORATIVE BOX, FOR WHICH WIRING INSTRUCTIONS ARE PROVIDED, CALLS FOR A BURIED CABLE, ONE THAT WON'T MAR THE PROJECT'S ELEGANT APPEARANCE OR TRIP YOU UP AS YOU AMBLE ALONG YOUR GARDEN PATH.

Suggested Tools

Table saw
3/8" Drill
1/16" Drill bit
No. 6 Pilot bit and countersink with stop collar
3/4" and 1-1/4" Forstner bits
Jigsaw
Fine-tooth laminate jigsaw blade
Tape measure
Try square
No. 2 Phillips screwdriver
Mallet
Palm sander
Staple gun

Cut List

Cedar is recommended for this project.

4	Sides	3/4" x 7" x 30"
2	Light base and bottom	3/4" x 5-1/2" x 7"
1	Top	3/4" x 7" x 8-1/2"

Hardware and Supplies

1/16" x 5-3/8" x 6-1/2" White acrylic diffusers (four)
2-1/4" x 5-3/8" Wire window screens (four)
No. 6 x 1-1/4" Deck screws
16-gauge x 1/2 Wire nails
5/16" Staples
No. 6 x 3/4" Panhead sheet-metal screws (six)
Outdoor-rated, surface-mount light fixture
Light bulb (25-watt maximum)
Type UF exterior cable
3/4" Galvanized pipe floor flange
3/4" x 12" Pipe (minimum length)
Exterior clear wood finish

Construction Procedure

1. Measure 2-3/8", 4-5/8", 6-7/8", and 9-1/8" from one end of each of the 30" sides (see Side Layout). Using a square, strike a line across each of the boards at those points.

2. To mark locations for the rounded edges of the slots in the sides, strike two lines between the 2-3/8" points and the 9-1/8" points, 1-5/8" in from each long edge. Using a 1-1/4" Forstner bit, drill a 1-1/4" hole at the thirty-two points where the lines intersect.

3. To make the four round-ended slots on each side piece, use a square to mark parallel lines between the outer edges of each pair of drilled holes. Then cut along the lines with a jigsaw.

4. Place a fine laminate blade in the jigsaw, and cut four pieces of 5-3/8" x 6-1/2" white acrylic to serve as light covers. Place a piece of acrylic over the lower three slots in each side. Center these diffusers over the openings. Use a 1/16" bit to predrill holes in the corners of each diffuser, and fasten each one in place with twelve 16-gauge x 1/2" wire nails.

5. Cut four pieces of 2-1/4" x 5-3/8" metal screen. Center these over the uppermost slots in the sides, and staple each one in place with six 5/16" staples. The screens should be placed on the same face as the acrylic diffusers.

6. Mount two side pieces to the edges of the remaining two side pieces, with the acrylic and screen facing in. Use a No. 6 pilot bit to predrill four holes along each edge on the two outermost sides, setting the depth stop at 1-1/4". Fasten the joints with No. 6 x 1-1/4" deck screws.

7. Locate the center of each 5-1/2" x 7" piece, and use a 3/4" Forstner bit to drill holes through both. Fasten the outdoor-rated light fixture over the hole in one piece, feeding the wire through the hole and securing the fixture with two No. 6 x 3/4" panhead sheet-metal screws. Slip this assembled light base and fixture inside the wooden housing, with the fixture and bulb facing up; place its upper surface 13-1/4" from the top edge of the housing. When the assembly is in place, predrill mounting holes through the sides and into the edges of the light base. Secure the platform with No. 6 x 1-1/4" deck screws.

8. Feed the wire (see the note that follows these instructions) through the hole in the 5-1/2" x 7" bottom piece, and then place the bottom in the lower end of the housing, recessing it 1/2". Secure it just as you secured the center piece, using No. 6 x 1-1/4" deck screws.

9. Place the 7" x 8-1/2" top piece at the upper end of the assembly. Using the No. 6 pilot bit, with the depth stop set at 1-1/4", predrill four pilot holes through this piece, centering each hole along one edge. Fasten the top to the sides with four No. 6 x 1-1/4" screws.

10. Sand the outside of the project. If cedar is used, the project won't require a finish, but several coats of an exterior clear wood finish will help to repel water.

11. To mount the project in the ground, first fasten a 3/4" galvanized floor flange over the opening in its bottom, using four No. 6 x 3/4" panhead sheet-metal screws. Thread a length of 3/4" galvanized pipe to the threaded flange, making sure that the pipe is a minimum of 12" long and threading the cable through it. Dig a hole in the ground, and place the pipe in it so that at least 6" of pipe stands above the top surface of the soil. Though this portion of the pipe will be visible, raising the project in this fashion is necessary in order to prevent water from seeping in through the bottom of the box. For added stability, use a 24" length of pipe, and sink it 18" below ground level.

 Note

If the light fixture is used outdoors and the electrical supply is fed from below ground, Type UF cable must be used to comply with the National Electrical Code. The connection between the feed wire and the wire from the fixture must also be code-compliant. If you are not familiar with local electrical codes, consult an electrician before installing this fixture.

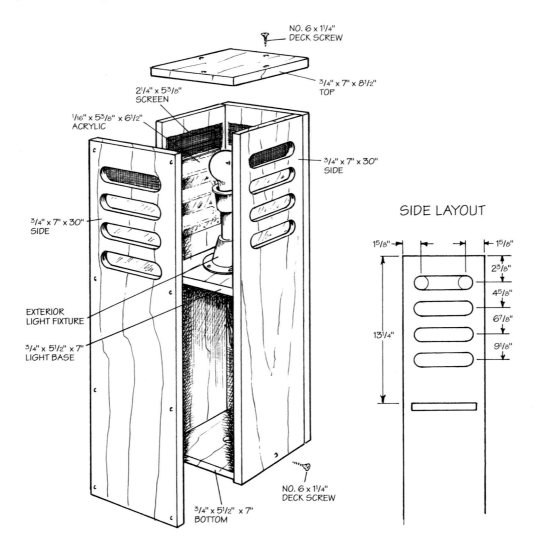

NO. 6 x 1¹/4"
DECK SCREW

³/4" x 7" x 8¹/2"
TOP

2¹/4" x 5³/8"
SCREEN

¹/16" x 5³/8" x 6¹/2"
ACRYLIC

³/4" x 7" x 30"
SIDE

³/4" x 7" x 30"
SIDE

EXTERIOR
LIGHT FIXTURE

³/4" x 5¹/2" x 7"
LIGHT BASE

³/4" x 5¹/2" x 7"
BOTTOM

NO. 6 x 1¹/4"
DECK SCREW

SIDE LAYOUT

1⁵/8"   1⁵/8"

2³/8"

4⁵/8"

6⁷/8"

13¹/4"   9¹/8"

Soil Sifter

Old hands will know how to use this project, but for those of you who have never seen one like it before, here's the trick. Place a wire-mesh screen into the frame and a tarp or sheet of plastic underneath it. Then shovel soil or compost onto the screen. Rocks, large roots, and other debris are sifted out, leaving you with fine-textured soil or compost for all your gardening needs. The two screens can be exchanged to yield either moderately coarse or fine soil.

Suggested Tools
Table saw
3/8" Drill
No. 8 Pilot bit and countersink with stop collar
Jigsaw
Compass
24" Straightedge

Tape measure
No. 2 Phillips screwdriver
Tin snips
Leather work gloves

Cut List
Pressure-treated pine is recommended for this project.

2	Rack sides	3/4" x 5-1/2" x 42"
2	Rack ends	3/4" x 5-1/2" x 28-1/2"
2	Legs	3/4" x 5-1/2" x 12"
2	Legs	3/4" x 5-1/2" x 24"
2	Tray supports	3/4" x 1-1/2" x 28-1/2"
2	Tray supports	3/4" x 1-1/2" x 39"
4	Tray ends	3/4" x 1-1/2" x 28-1/4"
4	Tray sides	3/4" x 1-1/2" x 38-3/4"

Hardware and Supplies
Waterproof wood glue
No. 8 x 1-1/2" Deck screws
No. 5 x 3/8" Wire cloth staples
No. 11 x 1/2" Double-point tacks
36" x 48" 1/4"-square Wire hardware cloth
36" x 48" 1/2"-square Wire hardware cloth

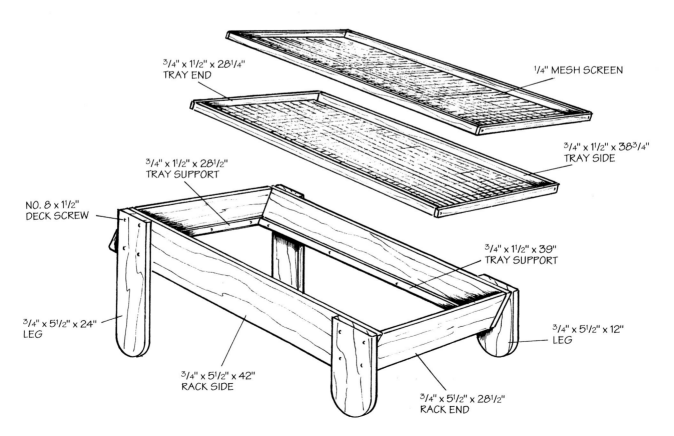

3/4" x 1½" x 28¼"
TRAY END

1/4" MESH SCREEN

3/4" x 1½" x 28½"
TRAY SUPPORT

3/4" x 1½" x 38¾"
TRAY SIDE

NO. 8 x 1½"
DECK SCREW

3/4" x 1½" x 39"
TRAY SUPPORT

3/4" x 5½" x 24"
LEG

3/4" x 5½" x 12"
LEG

3/4" x 5½" x 42"
RACK SIDE

3/4" x 5½" x 28½"
RACK END

Construction Procedure

1. Fasten the 5-1/2" x 42" rack sides to the 5-1/2" x 28-1/2" rack ends, using glue and three No. 8 x 1-1/2" deck screws, spaced 1-3/4" apart, at every joint. Predrill the holes with a No. 8 pilot bit, setting the stop collar at 1-1/2". The finished dimensions of the rack should be 30" x 42".

2. Glue and fasten the 1-1/2" x 28-1/2" and 1-1/2" x 39" tray supports to the lower edges of the box's interior, with the 1-1/2" faces meeting the frame. Use four evenly-spaced No. 8 x 1-1/2" deck screws on the longer supports and three on the shorter ones.

3. Set the table saw's miter gauge at 16°, and trim one end of each set of leg pieces. The longest edge of each leg should remain unchanged.

4. To round the ends of the legs, first locate and mark the center of each one at its square end. Then use a compass to strike a 2-3/4" radius from that point. Cut along the arcs with a jigsaw.

5. Place the two 24" legs at one end of the box and the two 12" legs at the other; their upper edges should be flush with the top edge of the completed rack. Fasten each leg in place with glue and four No. 8 x 1-1/2" deck screws. Each group of screws should be placed in a square pattern, 3-1/2" apart. Predrill the holes with a No. 8 pilot bit, setting the stop collar at 1-1/2".

6. Assemble each of the two trays by joining the 1-1/2" x 28-1/4" tray ends to the 1-1/2" x 38-3/4" tray sides with glue and one No. 8 x 1-1/2" deck screw at each joint. The completed trays should slide in and out of the rack without binding.

7. The two sections of 1/4"- and 1/2"-square hardware cloth should be trimmed to approximately 4" larger in each dimension than the trays themselves. Cut out a 2" x 2" piece from each corner, and fit the pieces into the two trays, folding the 2" widths of excess cloth up along the interior faces of the ends and sides of the trays. Bend the edges of the wire sections over the tray frames, and fasten them at the top with evenly spaced No. 5 x 3/8" staples. Inside the tray frames, use No. 11 x 1/2" tacks to secure the wire cloth.

8. The completed soil sifter needs no finish if it's constructed of pressure-treated lumber.

SEEDLING TRAY

When your seedlings are ready to be hardened off, place the individual containers or peat pots into this sturdy tray. If a late spring frost is predicted, just bring the entire tray indoors until the weather warms up again. The wire screen in this project will allow you to water your seedlings without drowning them, and the tray's size will save you multiple trips back and forth once your plants are ready to be set in their permanent locations.

Suggested Tools

Table saw
3/8" Drill
No. 8 Pilot bit and countersink with stop collar
1" Forstner bit
Tape measure
Tack hammer
Nail set
Palm sander
Tin snips

Cut List

Cedar or redwood is recommended for this project.

2	Ends	3/4" x 3-1/2" x 16"
2	Sides	3/4" x 3-1/2" x 25-1/2"
2	End retainers	3/4" x 3/4" x 17-1/2"
2	Side retainers	3/4" x 3/4" x 24"
2	End trim	3/8" x 5/8" x 18-1/4"
2	Side trim	3/8" x 5/8" x 25-1/2"

Hardware and Supplies

No. 8 x 1-1/2" Deck screws
18" x 30" 1/2"-square Wire hardware cloth
16-gauge x 1-1/4" Finish brads
No. 5 x 3/8" Wire-cloth staples
Leather work gloves

Construction Procedure

1. To mark locations for the finger holes, first locate the center of each 3-1/2" x 16" end piece. Then measure 7/16" to the right and left of the center-point, and mark. Connect the marks with a line drawn 1-5/8" down from the top edge.

2. Next, measure 1-1/4" to the right and left of the centerpoint, and mark. Connect the marks with a line drawn 1-1/2" from the top edge.

3. With a 1" Forstner bit, drill a 1" hole at each of these centers, four holes in each piece. Sand the end pieces smooth.

4. Fasten the 25-1/2" sides to the ends of the pieces just drilled, using two No. 8 x 1-1/2" deck screws, placed 2" apart, at each joint. Predrill the holes with a No. 8 pilot bit, setting the stop collar at 1-1/2". Sand the side pieces well.

5. Trim the hardware cloth to fit the bottom of the box. Making sure that the handle holes curve upward toward the top of the box, fasten the cloth to the edges of the assembled box, using wire staples spaced every 3" or so.

6. Fasten the retainer strips over the wire, using No. 8 x 1-1/2" deck screws (four in each side and three in each end) to hold the strips in place. Predrill the holes with a No. 8 pilot bit; set the stop collar at 1-1/2".

7. Any wire that extends past the sides of the box should be bent upward against the sides and ends of the frame. Place the side and end trim pieces in place, covering the seams and folded wire so that the trim will prevent sharp edges from snagging clothing. Fasten with 16-gauge x 1-1/4" finish brads, six per side and five per end.

8. No finish is required for this project; the wood should be sanded, however, to prevent splinter injuries.

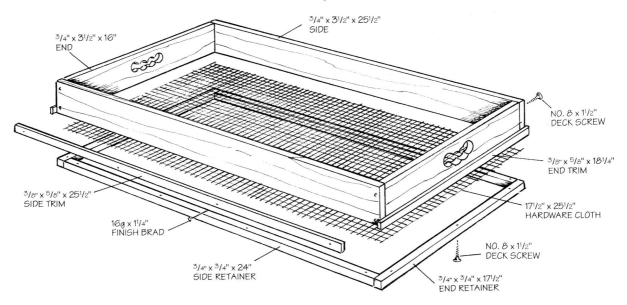

3/4" x 3½" x 16"
END

3/4" x 3½" x 25½"
SIDE

NO. 8 x 1½"
DECK SCREW

3/8" x 5/8" x 18¼"
END TRIM

3/8" x 5/8" x 25½"
SIDE TRIM

16g x 1¼"
FINISH BRAD

17½" x 25½"
HARDWARE CLOTH

NO. 8 x 1½"
DECK SCREW

3/4" x 3/4" x 24"
SIDE RETAINER

3/4" x 3/4" x 17½"
END RETAINER

REVERSIBLE BENCH

SAY GOODBYE TO ACHING BACKS AND MUD-ENCRUSTED KNEECAPS. WHEN YOUR PLANTS NEED LOVING CARE, BRING ALONG THIS HANDSOME PROJECT, AND SET IT UP NEXT TO THE BED OR BORDER WHERE YOU'LL BE WORKING. A QUICK FLIP TRANSFORMS WHAT LOOKS—AND ACTS—LIKE A BENCH INTO A COMFORTABLE AND CONVENIENT KNEELING SURFACE.

Suggested Tools

Table saw
3/8" Drill
No. 8 Pilot bit and countersink with stop collar
Jigsaw
Compass
24" Straightedge
Tape measure
Try square
No. 2 Phillips screwdriver
Palm sander

Cut List

Cedar, redwood, or pine is recommended for this project.

2	Legs	3/4" x 11-1/4" x 22-3/8"
1	Top	3/4" x 8-11/16" x 20-11/16"
1	Bottom	3/4" x 9-1/2" x 21-13/16"
2	Sides	3/4" x 4" x 21-3/4"

Hardware and Supplies

Waterproof wood glue
No. 8 x 1-1/2" Deck screws
1" x 12" x 24" Closed-cell foam pad (cut to size)

Construction Procedure

1. Though you won't use these marks just yet, start by marking locations for the top and bottom pieces on the 11-1/4" x 22-3/8" legs. Measure 2-1/2" in from one end of each leg, and strike a line across each board with a square. Then measure 8" from the same end, and strike a second line on each one.

2. Next, to taper the legs, find the center of the marked end of each one (see Leg Layout). Measure 4-1/4" to each side of this point, and mark. Use a straightedge to strike a line between each of these 4-1/4" marks and the corresponding corner at the other end of the leg. Cut along these lines.

3. To locate the decorative arcs in the legs, use a compass to strike a 2-3/8" radius from the centerpoint at the narrow end of each one. Then find the centerpoint at the wide end of each, and strike a 3-1/4" radius from that point. Cut the four radiused arcs with a jigsaw.

4. To taper the short ends of the 4" x 21-3/4" side pieces, set the table saw's miter gauge at 6°, and trim one end of each piece. Flip the boards over, measure 21-3/4" (along the long edge) to the opposite end, and trim that end of each board at 6°, too.

5. To bevel the long edges of the side pieces, keep the table saw's blade bevel at 6°. Rip both side pieces along their top (shortest) edge first. Before ripping the other edge, you'll need to determine the width of each finished side piece. Flip one over, measure up 4" from its longest edge, and mark (see Side Profile). Adjust the saw's fence to suit, and rip the lower edge so that the two edge cuts are parallel on the board.

6. Measure the top (short) edge of one side piece, and cut the top piece to the same length, leaving the saw blade at a 6° bevel and beveling both ends. (The length of the top's bottom surface should match the length of the top edge of the side piece; its upper surface will end up being slightly shorter.)

7. Measure the bottom edge of one side piece, and cut the top of the bottom piece to that length, leaving the saw blade at a 6° bevel and beveling both ends. (The underside of the bottom piece will be slightly longer than its upper surface.)

8. To determine the correct width of the top piece, measure the width of the legs at the upper lines marked in Step 1. With the saw blade still set at 6°, rip one long edge of the top piece. Then flip the top over, and rip its other long edge, also at a 6° bevel, so that its upper (shorter) width corresponds with the length of the upper lines marked on the legs. Repeat with the bottom piece, but remember that the width of its lower (longer) surface should correspond to the length of the lower lines on the legs.

9. Fasten the top to the side pieces so that the side pieces are recessed 1/2" in from the edges of the top. Use a No. 8 pilot bit set at a 1-1/2" depth to bore three holes, 9-1/2" apart, through the top and into the upper (short) edge of each side. Then attach the top, using six No. 8 x 1-1/2" deck screws and glue.

10. Place this assembly just below the upper lines marked on the legs. Using a No. 8 pilot bit, predrill three mounting holes through each leg and centered

in the ends of the top. Fasten the assembly with six No. 8 x 1-1/2" deck screws and glue.

11. Position the bottom against the legs and the lower edges of the sides. (The underside of the bottom should be placed just above the lower set of lines marked on the legs.) Predrill two sets of three holes, spaced 10" apart, as described previously, through the underside of the bottom and into the lower edges of the sides. Use six No. 8 x 1-1/2" deck screws and glue to fasten. For added stability, add six more No. 8 x 1-1/2" screws, three through each leg, centered in the short edges of the bottom.

12. Sand the entire project. Finish it with an exterior clear wood finish if desired. To make the seating (top) and kneeling (bottom) surfaces more comfortable, cut a 1"-thick closed-cell foam pad to size; place it on whichever surface you're using. Or cut two pads, one for each surface, and glue them permanently in place.

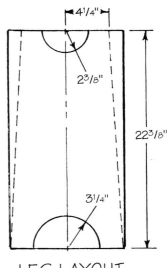

LEG LAYOUT

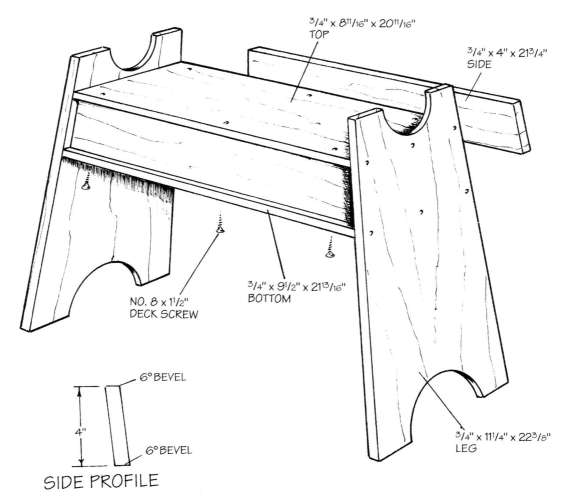

3/4" x 8¹¹/₁₆" x 20¹¹/₁₆"
TOP

3/4" x 4" x 21³/4"
SIDE

NO. 8 x 1¹/2"
DECK SCREW

3/4" x 9¹/2" x 21¹³/₁₆"
BOTTOM

3/4" x 11¹/4" x 22³/8"
LEG

6° BEVEL

4"

6° BEVEL

SIDE PROFILE

BOOT BENCH

Nothing takes the pleasure out of a satisfying day in the garden like the muddy boots and hand tools that tend to follow you indoors. Keep the mess where it belongs—out of your home but ready to grab next time you head for the backyard. Under the hinged seat of this project is a bin that will hold all those gardening extras. Toss in the dog's leash, the kids' toys, and the birds' seed, too.

BOOT BENCH

Suggested Tools

Table saw	1/2" Straight bit
3/8" Drill	Jigsaw
No. 8 Pilot bit and	Compass
countersink with	24" Straightedge
stop collar	Tape measure
No. 10 x 1/2"	Try square
Countersink	No. 2 Phillips screwdriver
3/32" and 1/8" Drill bits	Tack hammer
Router	Nail set
3/8" Roundover bit	Palm sander

Cut List

Cedar or redwood is recommended for this project.

2	Sides	1-1/2" x 11-1/4" x 16"
1	Seat	1-1/2" x 11-1/4" x 32"
2	Back supports	1-1/2" x 2-1/2" x 24"
4	Face boards	3/4" x 7" x 30"
1	Floor board	3/4" x 3-1/2" x 27"
1	Floor board	3/4" x 7-1/4" x 27"
1	Backrest	3/4" x 3-1/2" x 34"
2	Bottom supports	3/4" x 3/4" x 10-3/4"

Hardware and Supplies

Waterproof wood glue	No. 10 x 3" Deck screws
3" T-hinges (one set)	Tung oil (optional)
No. 8 x 1-1/2" Deck screws	

Construction Procedure

1. Lay one 11-1/4" x 16" side piece down with its best face up, and refer to the illustrations. On the upper 11-1/4" edge, mark 1-1/2" in from the right corner (which will be toward the front of the bench) and 3/4" in from the left corner (which will be to the rear of the bench). Use a straightedge to mark a line from each point just marked to the corner beneath it. Then locate the center of the lower edge, and use that point to strike a 2" radius in a half-circle pattern. Cut the two straight lines and the half-circle with a jigsaw. Sand the entire piece.

2. Select the best face of the other side piece, and repeat the procedure described in Step 1, but reverse the right-and-left placement of the 1-1/2" and 3/4" marks. Doing so will ensure that the two sides are symmetrical when the project is assembled.

3. On the inside face of each side piece, measure 13-

3/4" down from the upper edge, and mark a line across the board. Just above this line, place a 10-3/4" bottom support, one on each side piece. Fasten each support with glue and three No. 8 x 1-1/2" deck screws, drilling holes for the screws with a No. 8 pilot bit and setting the stop collar at 1-1/2".

4. Set the table-saw blade at a 5° angle. Run the 7-1/4" x 27" floor board through the saw to put a bevel on one long edge. Likewise, put the same 5° bevel on one long edge of one of the four face boards; this face board will be located at the upper front of the bench, and its widest surface will face inward.

5. Now reset the table-saw blade at a 3° angle. Put a bevel on one long edge of the 3-1/2" floor board so that it measures no less than 3-1/2" on its widest face. Also bevel one long edge of one more face board (the upper rear board) at 3° as well.

6. Position the two floor boards on the bottom supports so that their beveled edges are flush with the front and rear edges of the side pieces. Fasten them to the supports with No. 8 x 1-1/2" deck screws, two at each end. Before you drill the pilot holes, use a try square to make sure that the floor boards and bench sides are perpendicular.

7. Fasten the upper (5°) face board to the front edge of each side piece—top edges flush—using glue and two No. 8 x 1-1/2" deck screws at each end; space the screws 5" apart. Also attach the 3°-beveled face board to the upper rear edges of the side pieces in the same manner. Then fasten the remaining two lower face boards just below the upper ones, using glue and screws as before.

8. To locate the angles on each 24" back support, first use a straightedge to draw a line down its center. Then locate the center of this line, and use a square to mark a line across the support. Mark straight lines between the centerpoint at one long edge and the center marks at each end. Cut along these two lines with a jigsaw.

9. To locate screw holes on the back supports, mark points on the straight (back) edge of each one as follows: 7/8" and 2-3/4" from one end and 1-1/4" and 7" from the other end. All points should be centered. Use a No. 10 x 1/2" countersink bit to bore holes 1/4" deep at those points.

10. Measure and mark a line down the 3-1/2" x 34" backrest, 1-3/4" from one edge. On this line, mark points 1-3/4" in from each end. Using a compass

centered at each of these two points, draw a 1-3/4"
radius at each end of the backrest. Cut along the
lines with a jigsaw.

11. Use a 3/8" roundover bit in the router to round the
face edges of the backrest. Sand the board completely.

12. On the rear face of the backrest, make a mark 2"
in from each end. Align the back supports inside
these marks; their upper ends should be flush with
the top edge of the backrest. (The upper end of each
support is the one with the 1/2" bores closest
together.) Set the No. 8 pilot bit stop collar at 1-1/4",
and use it to drill through the bores and into the
backrest. (Be sure that the point of the bit doesn't
penetrate the front face of the backrest.) Glue and
fasten the backrest to the supports with four No. 8 x
1-1/2" decks screws.

13. Center the back assembly on the rear face of the
bench so that the lower ends of the supports are 8"
above the bottom of the bench. The sides of the supports and the sides of the bench should be flush. Use
a 1/8" drill bit to make a pilot hole through each
bore in the lower halves of the supports; make sure
that the bit penetrates the bench by at least 1".
Fasten each support to the bench with glue and two
No. 10 x 3" deck screws.

14. Set the table-saw blade at a 3° angle. Run the seat
board through the saw so that the front and rear
edges are beveled toward the top, and the bottom
face remains at an 11-1/4" width.

15. Use a 3/8" roundover bit in the router to round
the upper front and upper side edges of the seat, and
then sand the seat smooth.

16. Along the front edge of the bench, measure in 5"
from each end, and mark. Measure in another 2-
1/4" (or whatever width the squared leaf of your
hinges happens to be) from those points, and mark.
Use the straight bit in the router to mortise the edge
between these marks to a depth of 1/8". The hinges
will be placed in these mortised areas.

17. Fasten the squared hinge leaves to the bench
(with the screws provided), predrilling the holes with
a 3/32" bit. Then position the seat over the long
leaves, leaving a 1" overhang, and mark for placement. Remove the hinges from the bench, drill and
fasten the long leaves to the seat, and re-fasten the
squared leaves to the bench.

18. Give the project a final sanding, and apply several coats of tung oil, if desired, for a more finished
appearance.

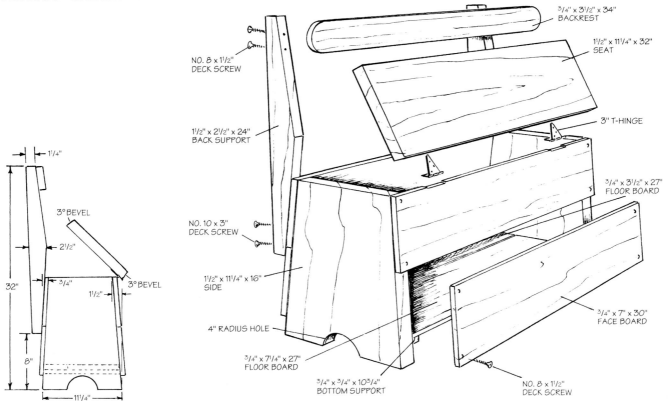

Bean Brace

This nontraditional brace is not only portable, but also makes a stunning showcase for flower-laden vines. Place it wherever your plants will get their required sunlight: against an attractive wall, in the center of your garden, even by the back door. The legs fold up for convenient storage, and the string leaders are easily replaced.

Suggested Tools

Table saw
3/8" Drill
3/16", 1/4", and 3/8" Drill bits
Tape measure
Mallet
Adjustable wrench

Cut List

Cedar, redwood, or pine is recommended for this project.

6	Supports	1" x 1-1/2" x 60"
1	Upper support	1" x 1-1/2" x 10'

Hardware and Supplies

Waterproof wood glue
3/8" x 3" Dowels (six)
String (nylon preferable)
1/4" x 2-1/2" Carriage bolts with nuts (three)
1/4" Flat washers (three)

Construction Procedure

1. Drill a 1/4" hole, 6-1/2" from one end of each 60" support, centering it on the 1-1/2" face.

2. Use 1/4" x 2-1/2" carriage bolts to attach the support legs together in pairs, securing them with flat washers and nuts.

3. Set the table-saw blade to cut a 20° bevel, and lock the rip fence at slightly more than 1". Run the narrow (1") edge of the 10' support piece through the saw. Then turn it around, and make a second pass on the opposite face to create a V shape, 1" wide at the top.

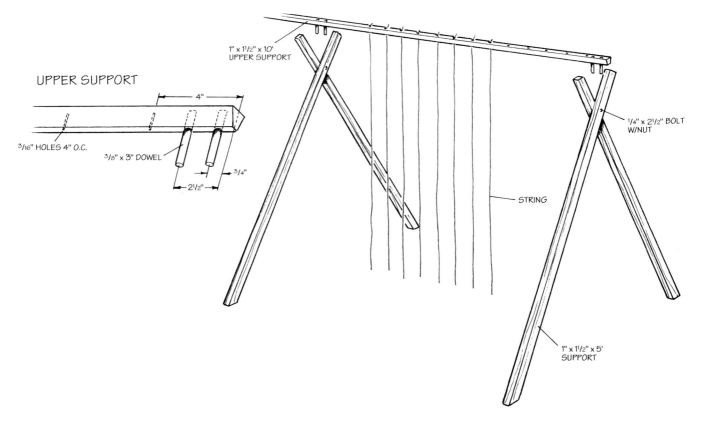

UPPER SUPPORT

1" x 1½" x 10'
UPPER SUPPORT

4"

3/16" HOLES 4" O.C.

3/8" x 3" DOWEL

3/4"

2½"

1/4" x 2½" BOLT W/NUT

STRING

1" x 1½" x 5' SUPPORT

4. Mark points 3/4" and 2-1/2" in from each end on the 1" face (see Upper Support illustration). To mark locations for the third pair of holes, locate the center of the support, and mark two more points 7/8" to each side of the center spot. Using a 3/8" drill bit, bore through-holes at each of the six points.

5. Mark points about 4" apart along the entire upper support (see Upper Support illustration). With a 3/16" drill bit, drill through-holes at each of these points. (Gardeners take note: You may want to adjust this spacing to suit your own planting needs.)

6. Glue the six 3/8" x 3" dowel sections into the 3/8" holes in the support so that the ends are flush with its 1" face.

7. Spread the support-leg sets to a 4' or greater width at their bases, and position them over the planting rows. Slip the upper support over one member of each set so that the dowels hold the supports in place and the bevel-cut edges of the upper support rest in the crook of each set.

8. Cut sections of string long enough to reach from the upper support to the ground, adding a few extra inches to each one. Tie a sturdy knot at one end of each length. Then insert the knot-free ends through the 3/16" holes; the knots will keep the strings from pulling through.

9. Neither cedar nor redwood needs a finish. Unfinished pine will last one or more seasons but will eventually deteriorate.

 Tip

Drilling a series of holes such as those for the strings in the upper support can be accomplished much more quickly by using a scrap of wood as a spacer guide rather than measuring and marking each individual point. Simply strike a centerline down the board, and rest the spacer alongside the last hole drilled to establish where the next hole should go.

HOSE WRAP

IT'S DIFFICULT TO FEEL ANGRY WHILE YOU'RE GARDEN-ING, BUT A KINKED OR TANGLED HOSE CAN TURN THE GENTLEST OF SOULS INTO A RAGING BEAST. PREVENT DANGEROUS PERSONALITY CHANGES, AS WELL AS DAM-AGE TO YOUR HOSE, BY BUILDING THIS HANDSOME STORAGE UNIT AND MOUNTING IT ON A WALL THAT'S CLOSE TO AN OUTDOOR TAP.

Suggested Tools

Table saw
3/8" Drill

1" Spade bit
Router
3/8" Cove bit
Jigsaw
Compass
Protractor
Tape measure
Try square
C-clamps
Mallet
Palm sander

Cut List

Cedar is recommended for this project.

| 1 | Face | 3/4" x 11-1/4" x 11-1/4" |
| 1 | Back | 3/4" x 11-1/4" x 20-1/4" |

Hardware and Supplies

Waterproof wood glue
1" x 7-1/4" Dowels (four)
1" x 6-1/2" Dowel
Exterior clear wood finish

Construction Procedure

1. Locate the center of the 11-1/4"-square piece, and strike an 11-1/4"-diameter circle around the board. Using the same center, strike a 9-3/4" circle as well. Mark horizontal and vertical centerlines across the face of the board.

2. Use a jigsaw to cut out the 11-1/4" circle. Sand the sides and edges, but leave the other pencil marks visible.

3. To locate the four upper dowel holes, use the protractor (and the center of the horizontal line as a base) to mark one point on each side of the 9-3/4"-diameter circle, 36° to either side of the vertical line (see Dowel Placement illustration). Then mark two more points, each 36° beyond the first set of marks.

4. To round the top and bottom of the 11-1/4" x 20-1/4" back board, first strike a centerline lengthwise down its center. Then measure 5-5/8" in from each end of the board, and mark on the centerline. Using a compass, strike a 5-5/8" radius from each of these points, one at each end of the board. Cut along the radii with a jigsaw.

5. Position the round face board over the oval back board so that the marked vertical line on the face board is parallel to and centered between the long edges of the back board and the top of the 9-3/4" arc is 4" from the upper edge of the back board. Clamp the two boards together at their sides.

6. Using a 1" spade bit, drill a hole at each of the four marked points on the 9-3/4" circle, through both clamped pieces of wood, to create four matched pairs of holes.

7. Mark a point 4" from the lower edge of the back board, on its centerline. Drill a 1" through-hole at this point.

8. Use a 3/8" cove bit in the router to rout around the face edges of both pieces of wood. Sand the edges and faces smooth.

9. Apply glue to the four 7-1/4" dowels, and tap them into the four holes in the back board. Also glue the 6-1/2" dowel into the hole at the bottom. That done, apply glue to the exposed ends of the four upper dowels. Then use a mallet to tap the face board over the four pegs until the ends of the dowels are flush with the upper surface of the face board.

10. Wipe away any excess glue, sand the assembled project, and apply several coats of exterior clear wood finish to keep water from being absorbed into the grain.

DOWEL PLACEMENT

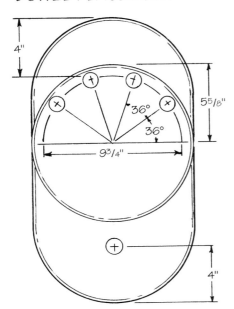

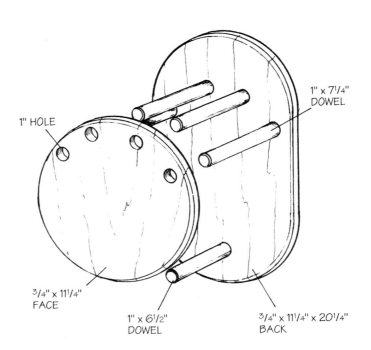

RAIL PLANTER

PLANT CONTAINERS PLACED ON PORCH AND DECK RAILS
SEEM TO HAVE A SPECIAL ALLURE FOR PROWLING CATS,
GUSTS OF WIND, AND MISCHIEVOUS YOUNGSTERS'
HANDS. IF YOU'RE TIRED OF HAVING TO SWEEP UP
SPILLED POTTING SOIL AND SHARDS OF BROKEN CLAY
POTS, SET ASIDE SOME TIME TO CONSTRUCT THIS
PLANTER. ITS FOUR SET-SCREWS GRIP THE RAIL SO
TIGHTLY THAT NOTHING SHORT OF A TORNADO WILL TIP
ITS CONTENTS OVER.

Suggested Tools

Table saw
3/8" Drill
No. 6 Pilot bit and countersink with stop collar
Tape measure
Try square
No. 2 Phillips screwdriver
Tack hammer
Nail set
Palm sander

Cut List

Cypress is recommended for this project.

8	Side rails	3/4" x 3/4" x 18"
6	End rails	3/4" x 3/4" x 8-1/2"
2	Ends	3/4" x 5" x 7"
2	Sides	3/4" x 5" x 18"
4	Spacers	3/4" x 3/4" x 1-1/2"

Hardware and Supplies

Waterproof wood glue
No. 6 x 3" Deck screws (for mounting)
16-gauge x 1-1/4" Finish brads

Construction Procedure

1. Butt the two 18" side pieces to the ends of the two
7" end pieces; fasten them with glue and 16-gauge x
1-1/4" finish brads, three at each end of each side
piece. The box should be squared and measure 8-
1/2" x 18" overall.

2. At the ends of the box, mount the four 8-1/2" end
rails to the top and bottom, using glue and 16-gauge
x 1-1/4" finish brads.

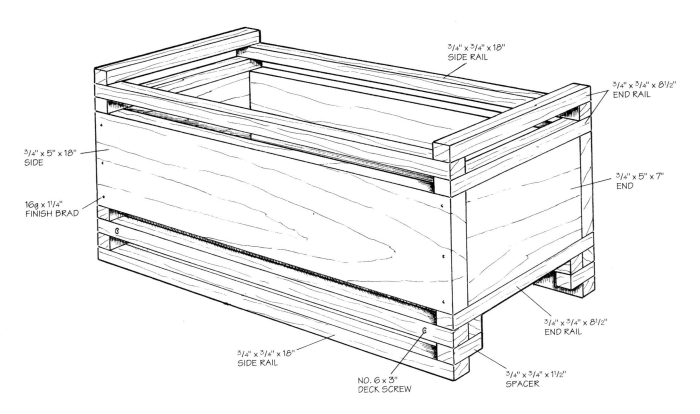

3/4" x 3/4" x 18"
SIDE RAIL

3/4" x 3/4" x 8½"
END RAIL

3/4" x 5" x 18"
SIDE

16g x 1¼"
FINISH BRAD

3/4" x 5" x 7"
END

3/4" x 3/4" x 18"
SIDE RAIL

NO. 6 x 3"
DECK SCREW

3/4" x 3/4" x 8½"
END RAIL

3/4" x 3/4" x 1½"
SPACER

3. Mount two 18" side rails on top of the rails just mounted, one over each side, at the top of the box only; fasten them with glue and finish brads. To complete the top of the planter, attach two more 8-1/2" end rails, using glue and 16-gauge x 1-1/4" finish brads as before.

4. Turn the box over, and mount a pair of 18" side rails over each end of the end rails already in place so that both pairs of side rails are flush with the end rails and with the ends of the box. Fasten them to the end rails with glue and 16-gauge x 1-1/4" finish brads, two per rail. Also place five brads through each inner rail and into each outer rail, to hold each pair of rails together securely.

5. Using the No. 6 pilot bit, adjusted for maximum depth, drill two holes through the side of each pair of rails, placing one hole at each corner (see the illustration). The screws in these holes will be used to mount the planter to the rail.

6. Mount a 1-1/2" spacer flush at each corner of the box, with their lengths running parallel to the end of the box. Fasten the spacers in place with glue and 16-gauge x 1-1/4" finish brads.

7. Using the same method as before, attach the final pair of 18" side rails to these spacers so that they're flush with the corners of the box.

8. No finish is needed for this project if cypress is used. A petroleum-based finish is not recommended since it may leach into the planting soil.

9. To mount the planter, fasten it to the rail with four No. 6 x 3" deck screws, placed in the predrilled holes in the side rails. (You may need to substitute longer or shorter screws, depending upon the width of your rail. If the rail is especially narrow, just add a third rail to the pairs described in Steps 4 and 5.)

10. Place your planting containers within the frame so that they rest directly on the rail.

SUNDIAL

FOR SERIOUS GARDENERS, WHO TAKE OFF THEIR
WRISTWATCHES BEFORE THEY GET TO WORK, AS WELL
AS FOR FOLKS WHO'D SIMPLY LIKE TO ADD
A DISTINCTIVE TOUCH TO THEIR GARDEN DECOR,
HERE'S A PROJECT THAT'S FUNCTIONAL, HANDSOME,
AND REMARKABLY EASY TO CONSTRUCT. IT TAKES
A BIT OF TIME TO LAY OUT THE NUMERALS ON ITS
FACE, BUT SURPRISINGLY LITTLE TO PUT THE
ELEGANT STRUCTURE TOGETHER.

SUNDIAL

Suggested Tools
Table saw
3/8" Drill
1/16" and 1/4" Drill bits
1-1/4" Forstner bit
No. 8 Pilot bit and countersink with stop collar
Router
3/8" Cove bit
1/4" Straight bit
Jigsaw
Compass
24" Straightedge
Tape measure
Try square
No. 2 Phillips screwdriver
Mallet
Tack hammer
Nail set
Palm sander

Cut List
Cedar or redwood is recommended for this project.

1	Post	3-1/2" x 3-1/2" x 60"
4	Strips	3/4" x 1" x 24"
4	Supports	1-1/2" x 3-1/2" x 3-1/2"
1	Dial	1-1/2" x 11"

Hardware and Supplies
Waterproof wood glue
No. 8 x 1-1/2" Deck screws
16-gauge x 1-1/4" Finish brads
17-gauge x 1/2" Finish brads
1/4" x 3-3/4" x 4-1/2" Black plexiglass
Plastic cement
5/8" Arabic numerals (1-8, 6-11)

Construction Procedure
1. The section of post that will be above the ground is 36" in length (see illustration). The remaining 2' of the 5' post will be buried in the earth.

2. Using a compass centered at one corner, strike a 2-7/8" radius on the face of each 3-1/2"-square support piece. Cut along the curved marks with a jigsaw, and then sand the supports smooth.

3. With the 3/8" cove bit in the router, cut a coved edge in both the right and left face edges of each

3/4" x 1" x 24" strip. Sand the strips smooth.

4. Position the four radius-cut supports at one end of the post, one centered at each face, and each flush with the top of the post. Use the No. 8 pilot bit, stopped at 1-3/4", to drill through the curved face of each support, 1-1/2" from the bottom of the support. Fasten the supports with four No. 8 x 1-1/2" deck screws.

5. Position one 24" coved strip beneath each support, centered on the face of the post. Fasten the strips with glue and 16-gauge x 1-1/4" finish brads, at least three in each strip; predrill the holes with the 1/16" bit.

6. To shape the dial, locate the center of a 1-1/2" x 11-1/4" x 11-1/4" section of wood, and scribe an 11"-diameter circle around it. Cut the shape with a jigsaw.

7. Use the 3/8" cove bit in the router to rout a cove into the upper edge of the best face of the dial.

8. Drill a 1/4" hole, 3/8" deep, in the center of the dial. Then, using a 1/4" straight bit in the router, cut a 3/8"-deep, 4-1/2"-long slot in the dial, one that extends from the centerpoint toward the outside edge. Sand the dial smooth.

9. Cut the section of plexiglass from corner to corner, creating a triangular gnomon (or style) with one 4-1/2" side and one 3-3/4" side. Use a 1-1/4" Forstner bit to drill a decorative hole in the triangle. Affix the gnomon to the slot with plastic cement.

10. Mount the dial to the assembled base by centering it over the four supports and lining up the gnomon with one of them; 1/4" of the dial will overlap at the ends of the supports. Use the No. 8 pilot bit to drill holes up through the supports, 1" from their outer ends. Then fasten the dial to the supports with four No. 8 x 1-1/2" deck screws.

11. Sink the post into its hole. At exactly 12 o'clock noon, level the post, and then position the dial so that the gnomon faces north, is directly in line with the sun, and casts no shadow. Fill the post hole with earth, tamping the soil down well.

12. Lay out the face of the dial according to the guidelines that follow these instructions. Each numeral should be tacked in place with a 17-gauge x 1/2" finish brad; predrill holes with the 1/16" bit.

13. Cedar or redwood needs no finish, although several coats of exterior clear wood finish will lend a pleasant patina to light cedar wood.

There's a mathematical method for laying out the numerals on the face of the sundial, one that takes your longitude and other factors into account. But a far simpler (though more time-consuming) way is to first set the completed project in place so that the gnomon points to the north and casts no shadow at 12 o'clock noon (standard time). Then, at every hour past noon, until 8 p.m., mark and place the appropriate numerals, according to where the shadow falls. Locate and attach the numerals from 6 a.m. to 11 a.m. the next morning.

Of course, the season in which you lay out the face of the dial has a bearing upon the distance between the numerals. Also, the implementation of daylight saving time (D.S.T.) will require that you add an extra hour to the time actually indicated on the dial. If you can live with the idea of your sundial being moderately accurate, you won't need to worry about the details.

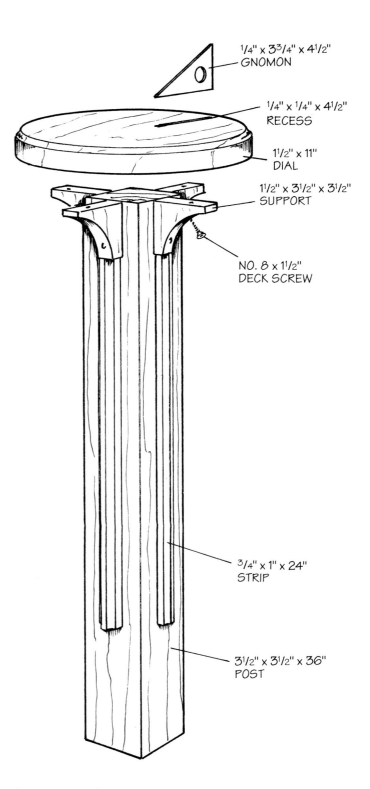

1/4" x 3³/4" x 4¹/2"
GNOMON

1/4" x 1/4" x 4¹/2"
RECESS

1¹/2" x 11"
DIAL

1¹/2" x 3¹/2" x 3¹/2"
SUPPORT

NO. 8 x 1¹/2"
DECK SCREW

3/4" x 1" x 24"
STRIP

3¹/2" x 3¹/2" x 36"
POST

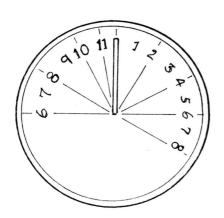

DRYING RACK

DRYING FRUITS AND VEGETABLES IS AN ECONOMICAL AND RELAXING WAY TO PRESERVE GARDEN PRODUCE, AND YOU DON'T NEED A FANCY ELECTRIC APPLIANCE TO DO IT. SET THIS PROJECT IN A WARM BUT SHADED SPOT, PLACE A LAYER OF SLICED FRUITS OR VEGETABLES ON EACH TRAY, AND COVER THE TRAYS WITH CHEESECLOTH TO KEEP AWAY HUNGRY BUGS. ALLOW THE PRODUCE TO DRY FOR A FEW DAYS; TO PREVENT MOLD, BE SURE TO BRING THE TRAYS INDOORS WHEN THE WEATHER IS HUMID.

Suggested Tools

Table saw
Dado blade
3/8" Drill
No. 8 Pilot bit and countersink with stop collar
Tape measure
Try square
Staple gun
Utility knife
Palm sander

Cut List

Cedar or redwood is recommended for this project.

8	Uprights and rails	1-1/2" x 1-1/2" x 48"
6	Tray supports	1-1/2" x 1-1/2" x 24"
6	Tray sides	3/4" x 1-1/2" x 24"
6	Tray fronts and backs	3/4" x 1-1/2" x 43-3/8"
3	Center supports	3/4" x 1-1/2" x 22-1/2"
6	Screen retainers	1/2" x 3/4" x 24"
6	Screen retainer fronts and backs	1/2" x 3/4" x 43-3/8"
3	Screen retainer centers	1/2" x 3/4" x 22-1/2"

Hardware and Supplies

Waterproof wood glue
No. 8 x 2" Deck screws
No. 8 x 1-1/2" Deck screws
No. 8 x 1-1/4" Deck screws
3/8" Staples
48" x 6' Nylon window screen

Construction Procedure

1. Install the dado blade onto the table saw, and set the depth at 3/4". Cut 3/4" x 1-1/2" dadoes into both ends of each 48" upright and rail.

2. The six tray supports will fit into dadoes cut in the uprights; in order to locate these dadoes, follow this step and the next one carefully. First, refer to the Drying Rack illustration. Then, on each of the uprights, mark the centers on the faces adjacent to the dado cuts that you've already made. (On two uprights,

make the marks on the face that is to the right of the cuts, and on the other two pieces, on the face to the left of the cuts.) Next, measure in 6" from each end of all four uprights, and mark lines on the same faces.

3. Measure 3/4" to each side of the center marks, and using a square, strike lines across the wood. Measure

1-1/2" further from the 6" marks, and strike lines.

4. Cut 3/8"-deep, 1-1/2"-wide dadoes at the indicated points, three on each upright.

5. Match the end dadoes of the uprights and rails to make the front and rear frames. The center dadoes

must face toward the inside of each frame assembly. Use a No. 8 pilot bit, with its stop collar set at 1-1/4", to predrill holes at each upright-and-rail joint.

6. Fasten each joint with a No. 8 x 1-1/4" deck screw and glue, squaring the frames as you proceed.

7. Fasten the 24" tray supports within the remaining dado cuts, using glue and a No. 8 x 2" deck screw at each joint; drive the screws through the uprights and into the supports. Set the pilot bit stop collar at 2". Square the assembly as you work, and sand it when you're finished.

8. Assemble each of the three tray frames by butting the tray sides against the ends of the tray fronts and backs so that the trays are 1-1/2" deep. With a No. 8 pilot bit set at a 1-1/2" depth, predrill holes through the tray sides and into the tray fronts and backs, one

hole at each corner. Glue the corners, and fasten with No. 8 x 1-1/2" deck screws. Place the center supports midway between the tray sides, and fasten them to the tray fronts and backs in the same manner. Sand the frames well.

9. Stretch the nylon window screen onto the first frame, and staple it in place. (Do not use galvanized screen for sun-drying; heat may cause toxins to leach into edibles.) Trim the excess screen off with a utility knife. Repeat this procedure with the remaining two screens.

10. Using 1-1/4" deck screws placed about 6" apart, attach the screen retainer fronts, backs, and sides over the stapled parts of each frame. Also attach the screen retainer centers over the center supports in each tray.

11. No finish is needed if cedar or redwood is used.

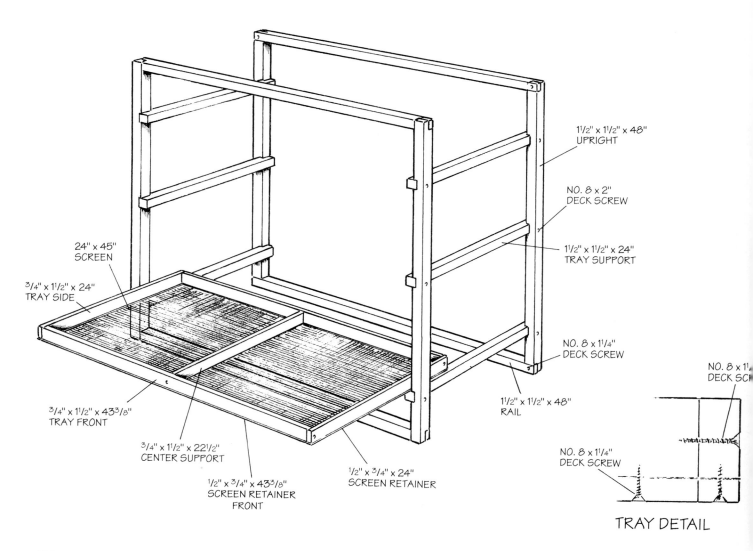

1½" x 1½" x 48"
UPRIGHT

NO. 8 x 2"
DECK SCREW

1½" x 1½" x 24"
TRAY SUPPORT

24" x 45"
SCREEN

¾" x 1½" x 24"
TRAY SIDE

NO. 8 x 1¼"
DECK SCREW

1½" x 1½" x 48"
RAIL

NO. 8 x 1¼
DECK SC

¾" x 1½" x 43⅜"
TRAY FRONT

¾" x 1½" x 22½"
CENTER SUPPORT

½" x ¾" x 43⅜"
SCREEN RETAINER
FRONT

½" x ¾" x 24"
SCREEN RETAINER

NO. 8 x 1¼"
DECK SCREW

TRAY DETAIL

FLOWER TRUCK

KEEP YOUR CUT FLOWERS FRESH BY
PLACING THEM IN THIS FLOWER TRUCK
AS SOON AS YOU'VE GATHERED THEM.
A HIDDEN CONTAINER OF WATER IN ITS
BASE WILL PROTECT YOUR GARDEN
TREASURES FROM PREMATURE WILTING, AND
ITS CONVENIENT HANDLE MAKES MOVING
FROM BED TO BED AN EASY MATTER. YOU
MAY EVEN WANT TO LEAVE YOUR BOUQUET
INSIDE THE PROJECT WHEN YOU'RE
THROUGH; IT MAKES A LOVELY VASE.

FLOWER TRUCK

Suggested Tools

Table saw
3/8" Drill
No. 8 Pilot bit and countersink with stop collar
1/2" Spade bit
Router
3/8" Roundover bit
Jigsaw
Compass
Tape measure
Try square
No. 2 Phillips screwdriver
Mallet
Hammer
Nail set

Cut List

Cypress is recommended for this project.

1	Back	3/4" x 6" x 22"
2	Sides	3/4" x 5" x 18"
1	Front	3/4" x 4-1/2" x 8-1/2"
1	Bottom	3/4" x 4-1/4" x 4-1/2"

Hardware and Supplies

No. 8 x 1-1/2" Deck screws
16-gauge x 1-1/4" Finish brads
Polyurethane

Construction Procedure

1. Measure down 3" from one end of the 22" back piece, and mark across the board. Locate the center of its 6" width, and intersect the previous mark. With a compass, and using the intersection point as a center, strike a 2" radius to make a 4"-diameter circle. Then, to round the upper corners of the back piece, use the same center to strike a 3" radius across the top of the piece. Cut along the 3" radius lines with a jigsaw.

2. With a 1/2" spade bit, drill a hole in the center of the 4"-diameter circle. Then start the jigsaw in this hole to cut out the circle.

3. To mark the cut-away in each 18" side piece, first measure down 6" from one end of each piece, and make a mark at the edge of the board. Using a compass, strike a 3-1/4" radius from this centerpoint to describe a quarter-circle between the edge below it and the middle field of the board.

4. Measure in 1-3/4" from the opposite edge, and mark the length of the board. This line should intersect the radius just drawn.

5. To curve the upper end of each side piece, measure down 1-3/4" from the top, and mark the edge from which you measured in Step 4. Use a compass to strike a 1-3/4" radius from that edge to the 1-3/4" line.

6. Use a jigsaw to cut along the marked lines, including the radii, to match the shape shown in the illustration. Trace the outline of the side piece that you've just cut onto the other 18" side piece; cut that one as well. Sand both pieces smooth.

7. Using a 3/8" roundover bit, round both faces of the inside edges of the hole in the back piece. Also rout both faces of the curved upper end of the back (see the illustration). Sand the back smooth.

8. Rout both faces of each side piece, from the top corner to the end of the large radius cuts.

9. Rout one 4-1/2" end of the 8-1/2" front piece, and sand the board smooth.

10. Butt the back piece to the edges of the side pieces as shown in the illustration. Using a No. 8 pilot bit, with the stop collar set at 1-1/2", drill three holes, spaced 7" apart, through each side of the back and into the edges of the side pieces. Fasten the pieces with six No. 8 x 1-1/2" deck screws.

11. Slip the front piece between the sides so that its face and the edges of the side pieces are flush. Using the No. 8 pilot bit, drill a pair of holes, 7" apart, through each side piece and into the edges of the front piece. Fasten with four No. 8 x 1-1/2" deck screws.

12. With a mallet, tap the 4-1/4" x 4-1/2" bottom into the base of the truck so that it rests flush with the bottom edges. Secure it with four pairs of 16-gauge x 1-1/4" brads, two each in the front, back, and each side.

13. Sand all parts of the assembly smooth.

14. For added protection against water, finish this project with polyurethane. To keep your flowers fresh, slip a water-filled can or plastic container inside just before you plan to gather your bouquet.

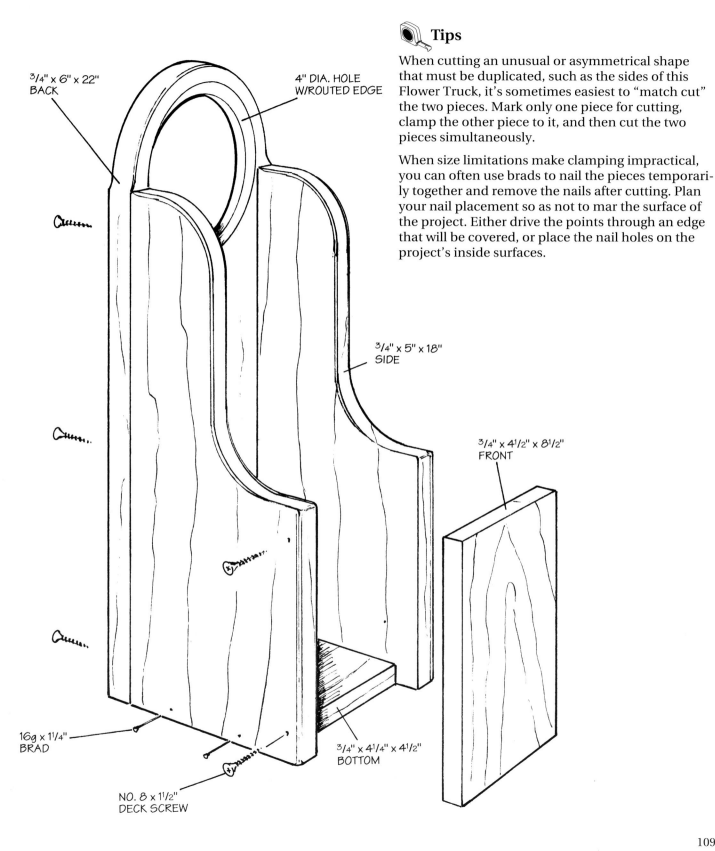

3/4" x 6" x 22"
BACK

4" DIA. HOLE
W/ROUTED EDGE

3/4" x 5" x 18"
SIDE

3/4" x 4 1/2" x 8 1/2"
FRONT

16g x 1 1/4"
BRAD

NO. 8 x 1 1/2"
DECK SCREW

3/4" x 4 1/4" x 4 1/2"
BOTTOM

Tips

When cutting an unusual or asymmetrical shape that must be duplicated, such as the sides of this Flower Truck, it's sometimes easiest to "match cut" the two pieces. Mark only one piece for cutting, clamp the other piece to it, and then cut the two pieces simultaneously.

When size limitations make clamping impractical, you can often use brads to nail the pieces temporarily together and remove the nails after cutting. Plan your nail placement so as not to mar the surface of the project. Either drive the points through an edge that will be covered, or place the nail holes on the project's inside surfaces.

TOOL-CLEANING BOX

BELIEVE IT OR NOT, FILLING A SIMPLE BOX FRAME WITH MIXED SAND AND MOTOR OIL IS A SURE WAY TO EXTEND THE LIFE OF YOUR EXPENSIVE GARDEN TOOLS. BY PLUNGING THE BLADES OF YOUR TROWELS, SHOVELS, AND OTHER OUTDOOR EQUIPMENT INTO THE CONTENTS A FEW TIMES, YOU'LL GIVE THEIR METAL SURFACES A QUICK SCRUB AND A RUST-PROOFING COAT OF PROTECTIVE OIL.

Suggested Tools

Table saw
3/8" Drill
No. 8 Pilot bit and countersink with stop collar
Tape measure
Try square
No. 2 Phillips screwdriver
Palm sander

Cut List

Cedar is recommended for this project.

4	Sides	3/4" x 11-1/4" x 16"
1	Bottom	3/4" x 9-3/4" x 11-1/4"
2	Bottom rails	1-1/2" x 1-1/2" x 11-1/4"
2	Bottom rails	1-1/2" x 1-1/2" x 6-3/4"
2	Top rails	1-1/2" x 1-1/2" x 14-1/4"
2	Top rails	1-1/2" x 1-1/2" x 12-3/4"

Hardware and Supplies

No. 8 x 1-1/2" Deck screws

Construction Procedure

1. Butt two 11-1/4" x 16" sides against the edges of the remaining two sides, with the top and bottom edges flush. Using the No. 8 pilot bit with the stop collar set at 1-1/2", drill four sets of three holes (as shown in the illustration), through the sides and into the edges. Space these holes 4-1/2" apart on each side.

2. Fasten the box together with twelve No. 8 x 1-1/2" deck screws. The assembled box should measure 11-1/4" x 12-3/4" when completed.

3. Place the two 11-1/4" bottom rails against the inside lower edges of the box, so that 5/8" of the width of each rail protrudes outside the edge of the box (see Bottom Detail). Use the No. 8 pilot bit stopped at 1-1/2", to drill two holes, 6" apart, through each side and into each rail, and then fasten the rails in place with four No. 8 x 1-1/2" deck screws.

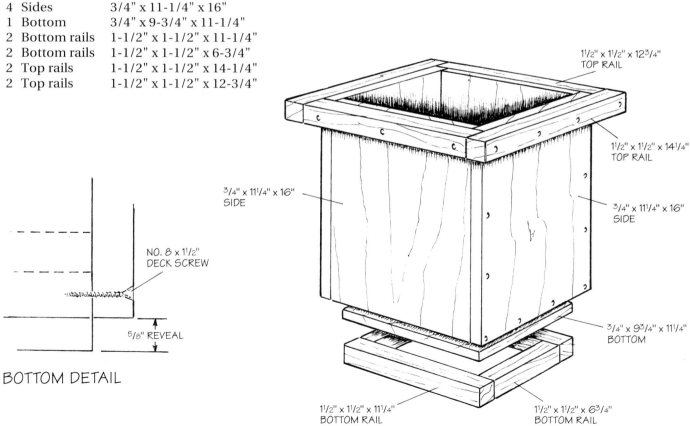

NO. 8 x 1¹/2" DECK SCREW

5/8" REVEAL

BOTTOM DETAIL

1¹/2" x 1¹/2" x 12³/4" TOP RAIL

1¹/2" x 1¹/2" x 14¹/4" TOP RAIL

³/4" x 11¹/4" x 16" SIDE

³/4" x 11¹/4" x 16" SIDE

³/4" x 9³/4" x 11¹/4" BOTTOM

1¹/2" x 1¹/2" x 11¹/4" BOTTOM RAIL

1¹/2" x 1¹/2" x 6³/4" BOTTOM RAIL

4. Place the two 6-3/4" bottom rails against the inside edges of the remaining two sides, and fasten them in the same manner.

5. Place the two 12-3/4" top rails against the outside of the wider sides of the box, flush with the box's top edges. Use the No. 8 pilot bit to drill three holes, spaced 5" apart, through the rails and into each side. Set the stop collar at 2" so that the screw heads will be well recessed. Fasten with six No. 8 x 1-1/2" deck screws.

6. Place the two 14-1/4" top rails against the outside of the remaining two sides of the box, and fasten

them in the same manner as the other rails. Use four screws in each of these two rails—two placed in the ends of the previously mounted rails and the other two spaced equally between them.

7. Sand the outside of the box, including the top rails.

8. Slip the 9-3/4" x 11-1/4" bottom piece into the box so that it rests on top of the bottom rails. (The weight of the sand inside will hold it in place.)

9. Fill the box to about 4" from the top with a mixture of sharp sand and a pint or more of clean motor oil.

COMPOST BIN

AMONG THE APPEALING QUALITIES OF THIS BIN ARE ITS SIZE, ITS GOOD LOOKS, AND ITS SIMPLE DESIGN, BUT ITS BEST FEATURE IS HOW IT WORKS. EACH OF THE FOUR, WIRE-COVERED FRAMES SLIPS EASILY IN AND OUT, SO WHEN YOU'RE READY TO TURN THE PILE OR GATHER SOME FINISHED COMPOST FOR YOUR GARDEN, YOU CAN WORK FROM ANY SIDE THAT YOU LIKE.

Suggested Tools

Table saw
Dado blade
3/8" Drill
1/8" Drill bit
No. 6 and No. 8 Pilot bits and countersinks
    with stop collars
Tape measure
Framing square
No. 2 Phillips screwdriver
Tack hammer
Tin snips

Cut List

Pressure-treated lumber is recommended for this project.

4	Posts	3-1/2" x 3-1/2" x 36"
8	Horizontal frames	3/4" x 3-1/2" x 43-3/4"
8	Vertical frames	3/4" x 3-1/2" x 36"
8	Wire retainers	3/8" x 3/4" x 31"
8	Wire retainers	3/8" x 3/4" x 36"
4	Bottom rails	3/4" x 3-1/2" x 48"
8	Braces	3/4" x 3-1/2" x 9-1/2"

Hardware and Supplies

Waterproof wood glue
No. 6 x 3/4" Deck screws
No. 8 x 1-1/2" Deck screws
No. 5 x 3/8" Wire-cloth staples
1-1/2" Hook-and-eye sets (eight)
20-gauge x 1" Poultry wire, 32" x 40" (four)
Leather work gloves

Construction Procedure

1. Two lengthwise dadoes (or rabbets) should be cut into each 36" post. This can be done with a dado blade or by making multiple cuts with the standard saw blade. In either case, 1" x 1-1/2" rabbets are cut into opposite corners of the post (see Post Detail). Because the posts

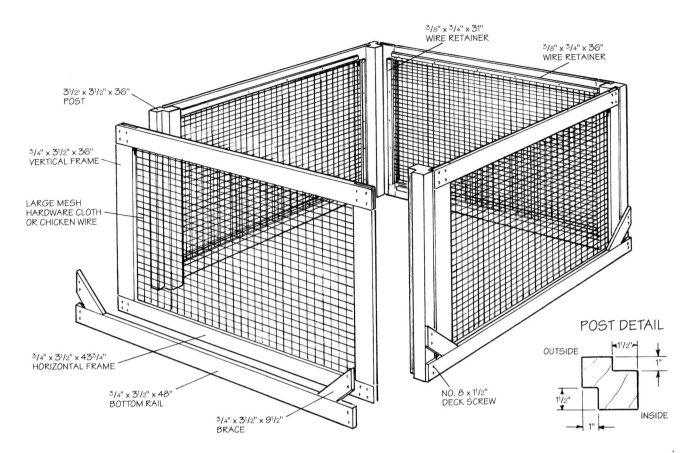

3/8" x 3/4" x 31"
WIRE RETAINER

3/8" x 3/4" x 36"
WIRE RETAINER

3½" x 3½" x 36"
POST

3/4" x 3½" x 36"
VERTICAL FRAME

LARGE MESH
HARDWARE CLOTH
OR CHICKEN WIRE

3/4" x 3½" x 43¾"
HORIZONTAL FRAME

3/4" x 3½" x 48"
BOTTOM RAIL

3/4" x 3½" x 9½"
BRACE

NO. 8 x 1½"
DECK SCREW

POST DETAIL

OUTSIDE

INSIDE

are each 3-1/2" thick, you'll probably have to remove the blade guard from the saw in order to allow the stock to pass through. Be extremely careful when using the saw without the guard; refer to the operator's manual before proceeding.

2. Try to construct the bin on the site where it will be used so that you won't have to move it once it's completed. Start by fastening the 48" bottom rails to the lower ends of the posts to form a 4' x 4' square. The rails should be flush on the bottom and edges with the bottom and sides of the posts, and there should be 44" between the shoulders of the dadoes on each side—the 43-3/4" horizontal frame will fit between these shoulders. Use glue and four No. 8 x 1-1/2" deck screws at each joint.

3. Trim the ends of each 9-1/2" brace to 45°, with the cuts in opposite directions. Fasten one brace at each corner with glue and No. 8 x 1-1/2" deck screws, taking care that the posts are squared up before driving the screws. Use two countersunk screws at each post joint, and two at each rail joint. When drilling the pilot holes at the rail joints, be sure to angle the bit enough to catch both wooden parts.

4. Use a dado blade in the table saw to dado the ends of the 36" and 43-3/4" vertical and horizontal frame pieces; each dado should be 3/8" deep and 3-1/2" wide to form half-lap joints. Assemble each of the four frames, using glue and No. 6 x 3/4" countersunk deck screws, four per joint. Make sure that each 36" x 43-3/4" frame is squared up before driving the screws.

5. Trim the poultry wire if necessary to fit on the inside of each frame. Fasten the wire to the wood with No. 5 x 3/8" staples, spacing these every 4" or so.

6. Fasten the wire retainer strips over the edges of each wire sheet, using No. 6 x 3/4" deck screws placed every 6". Set the stop collar on the No. 6 pilot bit at 3/4" when drilling the holes. If you happen to strike a staple, simply move the bit over slightly, and re-drill.

7. Slip the completed frames into the braced notches at the bottom corners of the posts. Fasten one hook-and-eye (not shown in the illustration) at each upper corner to hold the frames in place against the posts. Predrill holes for these with the 1/8" drill bit.

8. The completed compost bin needs no finish if it's constructed of pressure-treated lumber.

BARBECUE BOX

THIS ROOFED, OUTDOOR CABINET IS DESIGNED FOR FOLKS WHO PREFER TO SIT RIGHT BY THE GRILL OR BARBECUE PIT AS THEY COOK THE NIGHT'S DINNER. WHY RUN BACK AND FORTH TO THE HOUSE WHEN EVERYTHING YOU NEED—THE CHARCOAL, MATCHES, LIGHTER FLUID, GLOVES, AND LONG-HANDLED UTENSILS—CAN BE KEPT RIGHT WHERE YOU NEED THEM?

Suggested Tools

Table saw
3/8" Drill
No. 8 Pilot bit and countersink with stop collar
1/16" Drill bit
Router
1/2" Straight bit
Jigsaw
24" Straightedge
Tape measure
Try square
No. 2 Phillips screwdriver
Tack hammer
Nail set
Palm sander

Cut List

Cedar or redwood is recommended for this project.

2	Sides	3/4" x 7-1/4" x 32"
2	Back	3/4" x 11" x 37-1/4"
1	Gable end	3/4" x 7-1/4" x 22"
1	Center divider	3/4" x 7-1/4" x 34-1/2"
1	Bottom	3/4" x 7-1/4" x 20-1/2"
2	Shelves	3/4" x 7-1/4" x 9-7/8"
2	Roof	3/4" x 11-1/8" x 13-3/4"
4	Legs	2-1/2" x 2-1/2" x 6"
2	Doors	3/4" x 10-7/8" x 29-7/8"

Hardware and Supplies

Waterproof wood glue
1-1/2" x 1-1/2" Butt hinges (3 sets)
4" Slide bolt
1" Hook and eye
No. 8 x 1-1/2" Deck screws
16-gauge x 1-1/4" Finish brads
Exterior clear wood finish (optional)

Construction Procedure

1. To shape the 7-1/4" x 22" gable end, measure 2" from one long edge, and mark at both ends. Then locate and mark the center of the opposite long edge. With a straightedge, connect the two end points with the center one, and then cut along the lines with a jigsaw.

2. Lay the two 11" x 37-1/4" back pieces side by side, and place the point of the just-cut gable end at their top edge. The lower edge of the gable end should be 30" from, and parallel to, the lower edge of each back piece. Trace the outline of the peak on the gable end onto the wood beneath it. Then cut along the lines with a jigsaw.

3. Set the table-saw blade at a 25˚ angle. Trim one end of each 32" side to create that bevel. Then carefully pass one end of the 34-1/2" center divider through the saw so that half of its top edge is beveled. Turn the board over, and bevel the other half of the same edge so that the edge is peaked at its center.

4. To locate positions for the shelves, first measure and mark points 10" and 20-3/4" from the square end of the center divider. Use a square to mark lines across the board at those points. Then measure points 2", 12-3/4", and 23-1/2" from the square end of the right side piece, on its inside (longest) face. At these points, mark across the board with a square.

5. With glue and No. 8 x 1-1/2" deck screws, fasten the shelves to the center divider so that their lower edges meet the pencil lines. Use a No. 8 pilot bit, with the stop collar set at 1-1/2", to predrill two holes per shelf, 4-1/2" apart. Attach the marked side piece to the opposite ends of the shelves, using the same technique.

6. Then, in the same manner, fasten the bottom piece to the side and to the lower edge of the center divider, checking with a square to make sure that the corners are perpendicular. That done, attach the remaining side to the edge of the bottom piece, using glue and two No. 8 x 1-1/2" deck screws.

7. Join the gable end to the front of the box with glue and four No. 8 x 1-1/2" deck screws. Fasten at the center (with two screws) and at the side with the shelves (with one screw) first; the top point and the end should be aligned, respectively, with the point and side of the box. Check for square on the remaining side; then fasten that joint (with another screw) as well.

8. Fasten the two back pieces to the rear of the box with glue and No. 8 x 1-1/2" deck screws, spacing the screws 6" apart along the sides and bottom. To attach the boards to the center divider, use a 1/16" bit to predrill holes through the backs only, every 8" along the seam. Set 16-gauge x 1-1/4" finish brads into the divider.

9. Place the doors over the opening of the box, leaving a slight gap between them. Mark the position of the hinge leaves, spacing them along each door edge so that one leaf is in the center and the other two are centered 3-3/4" in from each end. Transfer the outline of the hinges to the edges of the cabinet. Then use a 1/2" straight bit in the router to cut a 1/8"-deep mortise at the place where each of the six hinges mounts. Predrill the hinge holes with a 1/16" drill bit.

10. Drill and mount the hinge leaves to the doors, using a 1/16" drill bit and the screws provided with the hinge sets. Then fasten the hinges to the edges of the cabinet, using the holes drilled earlier.

11. Mount the legs in each of the four corners beneath the cabinet, using glue and No. 8 x 1-1/2" deck screws fastened from the top or from the sides; use two screws for each leg.

12. Set the table-saw blade at a 25° angle, and trim both short edges of each roof piece to that angle; the angles should be parallel to one another on each piece. Fasten the roof boards to the cabinet so that the seam is directly in line with the center divider. Predrill holes through the roof boards with a 1/16" bit; then use glue and 16-gauge x 1-1/4" finish brads to fasten them to the center divider, sides, gable end, and back.

13. Sand the entire project, and apply several coats of an exterior clear wood finish if desired.

14. Fasten the slide-bolt eye to the upper right edge of the left-hand cabinet door, using the hardware provided. Match the position of the bolt assembly, and then fasten it to the gable end. Predrill all holes with a 1/16" bit. Attach a hook-and-eye latch to the center of the doors, midway between the upper and lower edges. For long-handled tools, add hooks to the inside of the left-hand door.

 Tips

Notice that the dimensions given in this project allow for tolerances between the two doors and between the top edges of the doors and the gable end. These slight gaps will allow the doors to open and close easily.

Placing a hinge leaf on the back face of a door can be a hit-or-miss proposition unless you measure carefully. You can reduce your chances of error if you first transfer the outline marks made on the cabinet edges to the edges of the doors after setting them up. Then use a try square to carry those marks as lines to the back faces of the doors. Measure in whatever distance the door-hinge leaves happen to be when they're attached to the cabinet, and mark that dimension on the backs of the doors. Don't drill all the mounting holes for each leaf at once—place one trial screw first, and then continue if everything fits properly. If it doesn't, you can easily move to another hole in the hinge leaf and try again.

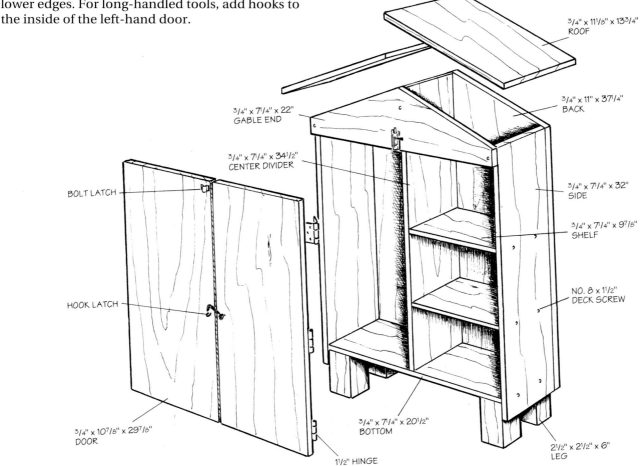

3/4" x 11 1/8" x 13 3/4"
ROOF

3/4" x 11" x 37 1/4"
BACK

3/4" x 7 1/4" x 22"
GABLE END

3/4" x 7 1/4" x 34 1/2"
CENTER DIVIDER

3/4" x 7 1/4" x 32"
SIDE

3/4" x 7 1/4" x 9 7/8"
SHELF

NO. 8 x 1 1/2"
DECK SCREW

BOLT LATCH

HOOK LATCH

3/4" x 10 7/8" x 29 7/8"
DOOR

3/4" x 7 1/4" x 20 1/2"
BOTTOM

1 1/2" HINGE

2 1/2" x 2 1/2" x 6"
LEG

SCARECROW FRAME

❧

THIS SCARECROW FRAME, WITH ITS ADJUSTABLE ARMS AND LEGS, COULDN'T BE EASIER TO MAKE OR MORE FUN TO DRESS AND POSE ONCE YOU'RE DONE. LEAVE YOUR GOOD TASTE IN CLOTHING BEHIND, AND INDULGE IN A FEW OUTRAGEOUS COLOR CHOICES. AND REMEMBER THAT A SCARECROW NEEDN'T BE MALE; A SKIRT THAT WHIPS IN THE WIND WILL KEEP THOSE GREEDY CROWS FROM THE CORN JUST AS WELL OR BETTER THAN ANY PAIR OF PANTS.

Scarecrow Frame

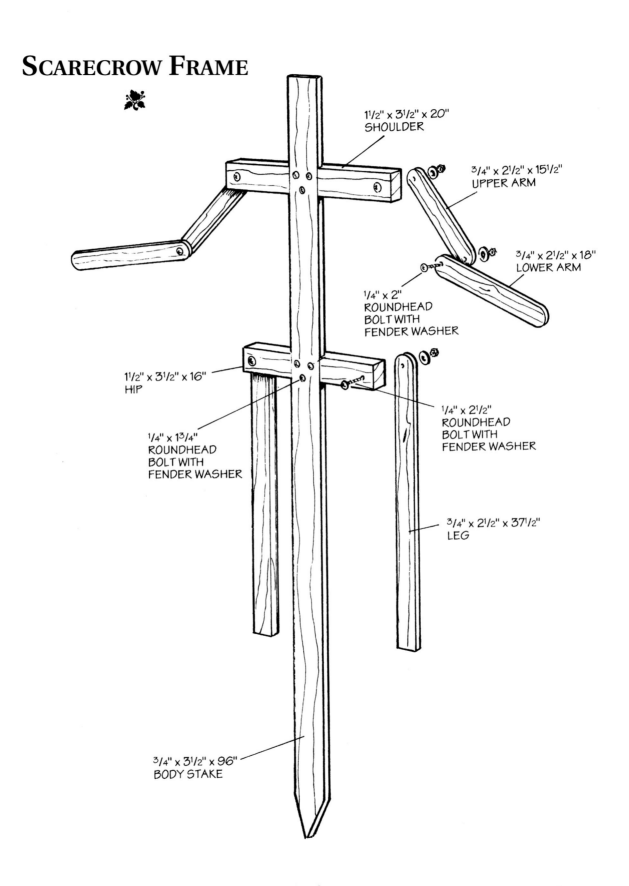

1¹/₂" x 3¹/₂" x 20"
SHOULDER

³/₄" x 2¹/₂" x 15¹/₂"
UPPER ARM

³/₄" x 2¹/₂" x 18"
LOWER ARM

¹/₄" x 2"
ROUNDHEAD
BOLT WITH
FENDER WASHER

1¹/₂" x 3¹/₂" x 16"
HIP

¹/₄" x 2¹/₂"
ROUNDHEAD
BOLT WITH
FENDER WASHER

¹/₄" x 1³/₄"
ROUNDHEAD
BOLT WITH
FENDER WASHER

³/₄" x 2¹/₂" x 37¹/₂"
LEG

³/₄" x 3¹/₂" x 96"
BODY STAKE

Suggested Tools

Table saw
Dado blade (optional)
3/8" Drill
1/4" Drill bit
Tape measure
Try square
Adjustable wrench
Palm sander

Cut List

Pressure-treated pine is recommended for this project.

1	Body stake	3/4" x 3-1/2" x 96"
1	Shoulders	1-1/2" x 3-1/2" x 20"
1	Hips	1-1/2" x 3-1/2" x 16"
2	Legs	3/4" x 2-1/2" x 37-1/2"
2	Upper arms	3/4" x 2-1/2" x 15-1/2"
2	Lower arms	3/4" x 2-1/2" x 18"

Hardware and Supplies

1/4" x 1-3/4" Roundhead bolts (six)
1/4" x 2-1/2" Roundhead bolts (four)
1/4" x 2" Roundhead bolts (two)
1/4" Fender washers (twenty-four)

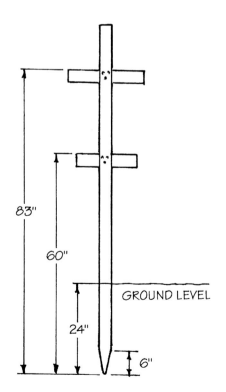

Construction Procedure

1. Beginning at one end, measure and mark across the 96" body stake at the following points: 6", 24", 60", and 83". To form a point at one end of the stake, first locate the center of the stake at the 6"-marked end, and then strike two lines from the center to the edges at the 6" line. Cut along the two lines.

2. Mark the center of the 20" shoulder piece, and measure 1-3/4" to either side of the mark. Using a try square, strike lines across the face of the board at each of these marks.

3. Set the table-saw blade at a 3/4" depth. Making repeated passes with it, remove the wood between the marked lines on the shoulder piece. A dado blade installed on the saw will accomplish this quickly and easily.

4. Repeat the same marking and cutting procedure to remove wood from the center of the 16" hip board.

5. Center and drill 1/4" holes, 1-1/2" in from the ends of the shoulder and hip boards.

6. Place the top edge of the shoulder at the 83" mark on the stake; place the top edge of the hip at the 60" mark. Drill three 1/4" holes in a triangular pattern at each cross-juncture, 1" in from the borders. Fasten the hips and shoulders to the stake with 1/4" x 1-3/4" bolts and washers.

7. Drill a 1/4" hole, 1-1/2" in from one end of each 37-1/2" leg. Drill a 1/4" hole, 1-1/2" in from both ends of each 15-1/2" upper arm.

8. Drill a 1/4" hole, 1" in from one end of each 18" lower arm.

9. Fasten the leg pieces to the hips with 1/4" x 2-1/2" bolts and washers. Attach the upper arm pieces to the shoulders with the same hardware. The lower arms are connected to the ends of the upper arms with 1/4" x 2" bolts and washers.

10. Choose leg and arm positions for your scarecrow, and tighten the movable-joint bolts so that the weight of the scarecrow's clothing won't affect the positions you've chosen. Don't over-tighten the fittings, though, or you won't be able to move the joints at all after the figure is clothed. Dress the frame, dig a hole, and using the 24" mark that you made in Step 1 as a guide, set the stake 2' deep in the hole.

Hose Guards

Any plant in the path of a moving garden hose is likely to meet an untimely end. Tame your hose, and protect your hard-won gardening victories by placing a few of these decorative and functional projects around the planting beds. They're guaranteed to keep wandering hoses from mowing down your favorite flowers.

Suggested Tools
3/8" Drill
1-1/4" Spade bit
Router
3/8" Roundover bit
Jigsaw
Compass
24" Straightedge
Try square
Palm sander

Cut List
Pressure-treated pine is recommended for this project.
1 Guard stake   3/4" x 3-1/2" x 13"

Hardware and Supplies
None

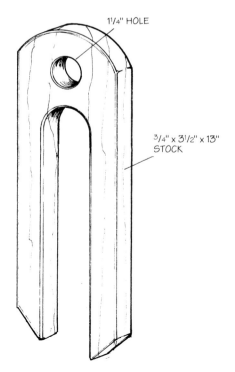

1¼" HOLE

³/4" x 3¹/2" x 13" STOCK

Construction Procedure

1. The instructions that follow will yield one guard. To shape the upper end of the guard, first strike a line down the center of the 3-1/2" wide stake.

2. Then, on this centerline, measure 2-1/4" in from one end, and mark. Place the point of a compass at this mark, and strike a 2-1/4" radius across the end of the blank.

3. To cut the hole, measure down 1-5/8" from the top of the marked arc, and use a 1-1/4" spade bit to drill a hole on the centerline at that point.

4. Measure 4" down from the top of the arc, and mark on the centerline. Draw a 1-7/8"-diameter circle (with a 15/16" radius), centered at that point.

5. At the bottom of the piece, measure 3/4" in from each side, and mark. Strike two lines, one from each outermost edge of the 1-7/8" circle, to the 3/4" marks at the bottom.

6. Using a jigsaw, cut along the radius line at the top of the piece, and then cut to remove the marked portion at the bottom. To make the guard easier to stake, trim a 45° angle at the bottom (and on the outer side) of each of the legs that you've just created.

7. Using a 3/8" roundover bit in the router, round all the edges of the project, and sand the wood smooth.

8. Treated wood needs no finish, though it can be painted if you like.

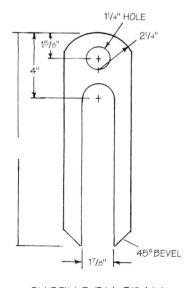

1¼" HOLE
2¼"
15/8"
4"
1⁷/8"
45° BEVEL

CUTTING DIAGRAM

FILE BOX FOR SEEDS

HAVE YOU EVER WASTED A GORGEOUS SPRING DAY
SEARCHING FOR LOST SEED PACKETS? WE HAVE. IN FACT,
UNTIL WE CAME UP WITH THIS HANDY SEED-STORAGE
BOX, SCRABBLING THROUGH KITCHEN DRAWERS AND
DUSTY JARS IN THE BACKYARD SHED WAS ONE OF OUR
MOST TIME-CONSUMING GARDENING ACTIVITIES. ONCE
YOU'VE BUILT THIS SIMPLE PROJECT, YOU'LL KNOW
RIGHT WHERE TO LOOK WHEN IT'S TIME TO PLANT.

Suggested Tools
- Table saw
- Tape measure
- Try square
- Tack hammer
- Nail set
- Palm sander

Cut List
Cedar or pine is recommended for this project.

Qty	Part	Dimensions
2	Lower ends	1/2" x 3-1/4" x 5"
4	Upper ends	1/2" x 2-1/2" x 12-3/4"
2	Lower sides	1/2" x 3-1/4" x 12"
2	Upper sides	1/2" x 2-3/4" x 12"
1	Base	1/2" x 5" x 13"
2	Top	1/2" x 2-1/2" x 13"
2	Dividers	1/2" x 3-1/4" x 4"

Hardware and Supplies

    Yellow glue
    1" x 1-1/4" Decorative flush-mount hinges
      (two sets)
    16-gauge x 1-1/4" Finish brads
    Tung oil (optional)

Construction Procedure

1. Butt the lower ends to the lower sides so that the upper and lower edges are flush. Glue and fasten the joints using 16-gauge x 1-1/4" finish brads.

2. Position the base over the bottom edge of the assembled frame, and fasten it with glue and 16-gauge x 1-1/4" finish brads.

3. Measure 4" in from each inside end, and mark on the inside surfaces of the side pieces. Center the two 3-1/4" x 4" dividers over the marks, and fasten them by setting 16-gauge x 1-1/4" finish brads through the sides and bottom.

4. Butt two upper ends to one of the upper sides so that the pieces are square; check with a try square. The upper and lower edges should be flush. Glue and fasten the side to the end pieces with 16-gauge x 1-1/4" finish brads. Repeat with the other side and end pieces.

5. With glue and 16-gauge x 1-1/4" finish brads, fasten a top piece to each side-and-end piece assembly so that the outside edges are flush.

6. Sand all parts of the box. Then place the two top assemblies in place—open sides toward the center—to check for fit.

7. Use one set of hinges on each side to connect the tops to the box bottom. Center these hinges 6" apart, and fasten them with the finish brads supplied with the hinge sets.

8. For a more finished appearance, wipe the wood with several coats of tung oil.

 ## Tip

With a bit of planning, you can shorten the construction of this File Box project by assembling the entire top as one unit rather than two separate ones. Simply allow an extra 1/8" in overall width to compensate for the saw kerf, and make sure that you don't place any brads in the center of the top piece. Then measure very carefully, and run the completed assembly through your table saw to split it cleanly down the middle.

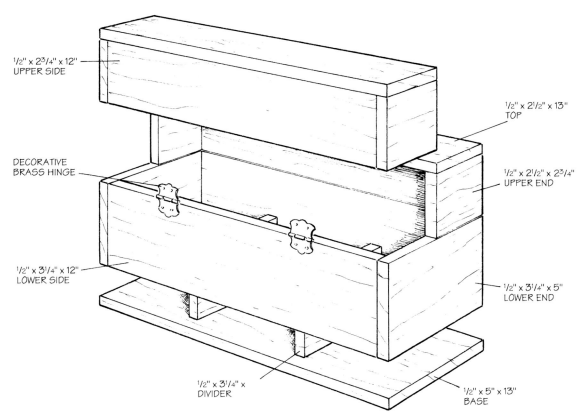

1/2" x 2³/4" x 12"
UPPER SIDE

1/2" x 2¹/2" x 13"
TOP

DECORATIVE
BRASS HINGE

1/2" x 2¹/2" x 2³/4"
UPPER END

1/2" x 3¹/4" x 12"
LOWER SIDE

1/2" x 3¹/4" x 5"
LOWER END

1/2" x 3¹/4" x
DIVIDER

1/2" x 5" x 13"
BASE

PORTABLE SHADE SCREENS

IF YOUR OUTDOOR LOUNGING AREAS ARE LIMITED BY
LACK OF SHADE, YOU'LL DEFINITELY WANT TO TRY THIS
SIMPLE PROJECT. TWO OR THREE OF THESE DISTINCTIVE
SLATTED FRAMES WILL LET YOU CREATE LUXURIOUS
COOL SPOTS WHEREVER YOU WANT THEM. THE SCREENS
MAKE MARVELOUS TRELLISES, TOO; JUST ANCHOR THEM
IN PLACE BEFORE SETTING OUT YOUR CLIMBING PLANTS.

Suggested Tools

Table saw
Circular saw
3/8" Drill
No. 8 Pilot bit and countersink with stop collar
Tape measure
Try square
24" Straightedge
No. 2 Phillips screwdriver
Tack hammer
Nail set
Palm sander

Cut List

Cypress or redwood is recommended for this project.

10	Vertical slats	3/4" x 1" x 84"
4	Center braces	3/4" x 1-3/8" x 18"
2	Top braces	3/4" x 2-1/2" x 18"
2	Bottom braces	3/4" x 3-1/4" x 18"
2	Feet	3/4" x 2-3/4" x 30"
1	Spacer	3/4" x 7/8" x 12"

Hardware and Supplies

Waterproof wood glue
3" Corner braces (four)
No. 8 x 3/4" Galvanized flathead screws
16-gauge x 1-1/4" Finish brads
Exterior clear wood finish

Construction Procedure

1. Sand all the individual pieces before you start the
assembly process. Lay one 2-1/2" x 18" top brace
and one 3-1/4" x 18" bottom brace on a flat surface,
parallel to each other and spaced so that their outside edges are 84" apart. Place a 1" x 84" vertical slat,
broad side down, at each end of the braces, flush
with their ends and edges. Glue these two outer slats
to the braces, square them, and secure them with
16-gauge x 1-1/4" finish brads.

2. Using the 7/8" x 12" piece of wood as a spacer gauge, position the eight remaining slats across the two braces so that all slats are 7/8" apart. Fasten them just as you fastened the slats in Step 1.

3. Turn the assembly over, and use glue and finish brads to fasten the other set of top and bottom braces.

4. Using a straightedge, strike a line across both the front and back of the slats, 24" up from the top edge of the bottom brace. Strike two more lines on the fronts and backs of the slats, 14" down from the lower edge of the top brace. Then use glue and 16-gauge x 1-1/4" finish brads to fasten the 1-3/8" x 18" center braces; their ends should rest flush with the edges of the outer slats, and their edges should be even with the marked lines. The upper set of center braces fastens below the upper lines, and the lower set fastens above the lower lines.

5. With a square, strike lines across the centers of the 2-3/4" x 30" feet. Measure 1-1/8" to each side of these centerlines, and strike a second and third set of lines.

6. Fasten a pair of 3" corner braces to each side of the bottom brace; position them so that they line up with the second slat in from each side and are flush with the bottom of the wooden brace. Predrill the holes with a No. 8 pilot bit, and secure the braces with No. 8 x 3/4" galvanized flathead screws.

7. Position the assembled screen between the marked lines on the feet. Center the corner braces on the feet, and fasten them with No. 8 x 3/4" galvanized flathead screws.

8. The screen needs no finish if it's made of cypress or redwood.

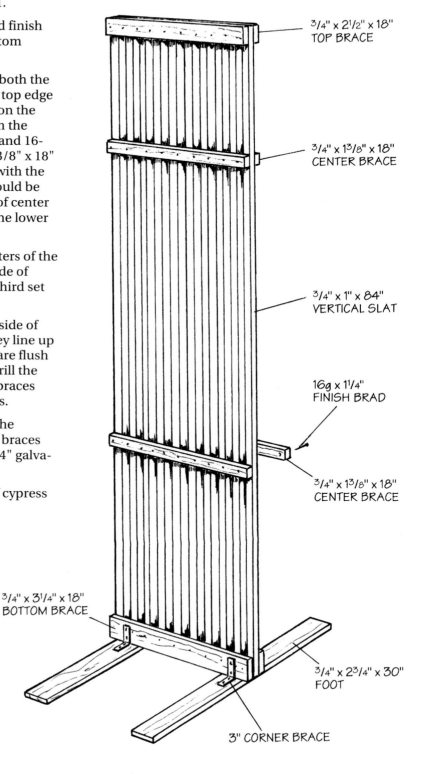

3/4" x 2½" x 18"
TOP BRACE

3/4" x 1⅜" x 18"
CENTER BRACE

3/4" x 1" x 84"
VERTICAL SLAT

16g x 1¼"
FINISH BRAD

3/4" x 1⅜" x 18"
CENTER BRACE

3/4" x 3¼" x 18"
BOTTOM BRACE

3/4" x 2¾" x 30"
FOOT

3" CORNER BRACE

COLD FRAME

EXTENDING THE GROWING SEASON IS AN EASY MATTER WITH THIS SIMPLE PROJECT. JUMP-START YOUR EARLY SEEDLINGS BY SETTING THEM IN THE FRAME A FEW WEEKS BEFORE YOUR LAST SPRING FROST DATE. ON CHILLY DAYS, THE LID SHOULD BE KEPT CLOSED; ON WARMER ONES, THE NOTCHED GLIDERS WILL PROP THE LID UP AT JUST THE RIGHT HEIGHT TO KEEP YOUR PLANTS COMFORTABLE.

Suggested Tools
Table saw
Dado blade
3/8" Drill
No. 8 Pilot bit and countersink with stop collar
Jigsaw
Compass
24" Straightedge
Tape measure
3/4" Chisel
Tack hammer
Nail set
No. 2 Phillips screwdriver
Staple gun

Cut List

An exterior-grade C-D plywood and cedar, redwood, or pine is recommended for this project.

1	Front	3/4" x 12" x 48"
1	Back	3/4" x 18" x 48"
2	Sides	3/4" x 18" x 28-1/2"
2	Back posts	1-1/2" x 1-1/2" x 17-3/8"
2	Front posts	1-1/2" x 1-1/2" x 11-3/4"
2	Prop arms	3/4" x 1-1/2" x 20"
1	Prop-arm connector	3/4" x 1-1/2" x 42-1/4"
1	Prop-arm stop	3/4" x 1-1/2" x 46-1/2"
2	Frame front and back	1-1/2" x 2-1/2" x 49"
2	Frame sides	1-1/2" x 2-1/2" x 31"
2	Frame centers	3/4" x 1-1/2" x 27-1/2"
2	Front and rear trim	3/8" x 3/4" x 45-3/4"
4	Side and center trim	3/8" x 3/4" x 26"

Hardware and Supplies

Waterproof wood glue
3" T-hinges (one set)
No. 8 x 1-1/2" Deck screws
16-gauge x 1-1/4" Finish brads
No. 8 x 1-1/2" Roundhead wood screws (two)
3/16" Flat washers (two)
Clear polyethylene (6 mm), 27-1/2" x 45-3/4"
Exterior latex paint

Construction Procedure

1. To lay out the plywood sides, first cut a piece of plywood to 28-1/2" x 30" in size. Then measure 12" down one 30" edge, and mark. Measure 18" down the opposite edge, and mark. Use a straightedge to draw a line between the two marks, and cut along the line with a jigsaw to make the two separate sides.

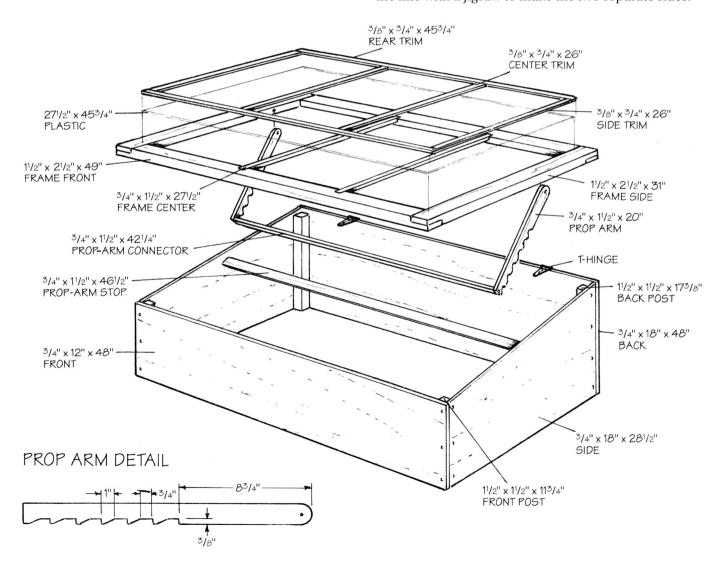

3/8" x 3/4" x 45 3/4"
REAR TRIM

3/8" x 3/4" x 26"
CENTER TRIM

27 1/2" x 45 3/4"
PLASTIC

3/8" x 3/4" x 26"
SIDE TRIM

1 1/2" x 2 1/2" x 49"
FRAME FRONT

3/4" x 1 1/2" x 27 1/2"
FRAME CENTER

1 1/2" x 2 1/2" x 31"
FRAME SIDE

3/4" x 1 1/2" x 42 1/4"
PROP-ARM CONNECTOR

3/4" x 1 1/2" x 20"
PROP ARM

3/4" x 1 1/2" x 46 1/2"
PROP-ARM STOP

T-HINGE

1 1/2" x 1 1/2" x 17 3/8"
BACK POST

3/4" x 18" x 48"
BACK

3/4" x 12" x 48"
FRONT

3/4" x 18" x 28 1/2"
SIDE

1 1/2" x 1 1/2" x 11 3/4"
FRONT POST

PROP ARM DETAIL

1"   3/4"   8 3/4"

3/8"

128

2. Set the table-saw blade at a 12° angle, and rip one long edge of the 12"-wide front and the 18"-wide back. Rip each panel so that it retains its original width and its best face will be toward the outside of the finished frame.

3. Fasten an 11-3/4" front post and a 17-3/8" back post to each side piece so that the posts are flush with the bottom edges of the side pieces. The posts should be attached with glue and No. 8 x 1-1/2" deck screws, countersunk from the outside, to the secondary (poorest) face of the plywood.

4. In the same manner, attach the front and back sections to the posts on each side piece. Make sure that the bevels are facing toward the front of the frame.

5. Using a dado blade on the table saw, cut 3/4"-deep, 2-1/2"-wide dadoes into the ends of the frame front, back, and side pieces. Be sure to cut both dadoes on the same face of each piece.

6. To establish the placement of the two 27-1/2" frame centers, temporarily lay out the frame. Measure in 16-1/2" from the outside edge of each frame side, and mark on the inside edge of the frame front and back. Then measure another 3/4" inward from those points, and mark again. Place the two frame centers between the marked lines, and mark the front and back at the ends of the frame centers.

7. Set the dado blade to cut at whatever depth the marked slots happen to be. The blade should be adjusted at a 3/4" width. Cut slots into the front and back frame pieces where indicated.

8. Glue and nail the frame pieces together using 16-gauge x 1-1/4" finish brads and making sure that the slots face one another. Then glue the frame centers into the slots, and secure them with finish brads set in from the edges of the frame.

9. Mark each of the 1-1/2" x 20" prop arms as follows (see Prop Arm Detail): Measure 3/4" from one end, and mark in the center. Measure 8-3/4" from the same end, and mark across the arm. Then measure and mark a line along the arm, 3/8" from the lower edge; use a straightedge to mark this line. Next, measuring from the point where the two lines intersect, measure and make the following marks: 3/4", 1", 3/4", 1", and so on until a total of six 3/4" blocks are marked. Draw short diagonal lines between each 3/4" mark on the 3/8" line and the next 1" mark on the edge of the arm, as shown in the illustration.

10. With a compass, scribe a 3/4" radius at the end of the arm, using the first mark as a center, and then cut the radius with a jigsaw. Go on to cut the back side and diagonal of each block to make a total of six notches in the edge of the arm. Drill a 3/16" hole at the center mark on the radiused end. Repeat these procedures on the other prop arm.

11. Using the No. 8 pilot bit, drill a hole through the center of each frame side edge, 5" from the inside edge of the back piece. Then attach the 46-1/2" prop-arm stop to the inside faces of the plywood side, 1-3/4" from the top edge and 14" from the back, using glue and a No. 8 x 1-1/2" deck screw in each end. The stop should be set at an angle so that its edge will catch the prop arms squarely.

12. Attach the completed frame to the back piece of plywood with two 3" T-hinges set 9" in from the outside corners. Use the hardware provided with the hinges; no mortise cuts are needed to set the hinge leaves.

13. Fasten the prop arms to the ends of the 42-1/4" prop-arm connector, using glue and two No. 8 x 1-1/2" deck screws per joint. Then use the No. 8 x 2-1/2" roundhead wood screws and 3/16" flat washers to secure the pivoting ends of the arms to the holes already drilled in the inside edges of the frame.

14. Sand the exterior of the frame. Prime and paint the wooden surfaces, including the as-yet-unfastened trim strips.

15. Cut the polyethylene film to rough dimensions, and staple it over the frame opening. Cover the edges with the painted trim strips, and fasten the strips using 16-gauge x 1-1/4" finish brads. Set the nail heads just below the surface of the wood.

16. The cold frame can be insulated on the inside by cutting pieces of extruded styrene insulation board to fit. If cost isn't a consideration, you may want to replace the polyethylene with tempered glass; if you do this, the glass should be set in a 1/4"-deep, 3/4"-wide routed mortise, on a bed of glazing putty or silicone. It can be held in place with a 1-1/2" trim strip that is fastened to the frame with No. 6 x 1" roundhead wood screws.

BOOTJACK—AND BRUSH

❧

MUDDY BOOTS AREN'T ANY FUN. THEY'RE DIFFI-
CULT TO TAKE OFF BY HAND, AND THEY'RE TIME-
CONSUMING TO CLEAN ONCE THE MUD HAS CAKED
AND DRIED. BUT ONCE YOU'VE BUILT THIS PROJECT,
YOU'LL NO LONGER HAVE TO ENGAGE IN FURIOUS
BATTLE WITH YOUR GARDENING FOOTWEAR. WHEN
YOU REACH THE BACK DOOR, RUN YOUR BOOT
THROUGH ITS BRUSHES TWO OR THREE TIMES. THEN
SLIP THE HEEL INTO THE V-SHAPED SLOT. PULL
UP—AND PRESTO—THE CLEANED BOOT SLIPS OFF.

Suggested Tools

Table saw
3/8" Drill
No. 6 Pilot bit and countersink with stop collar
Jigsaw
Compass
Tape measure
Try square
No. 2 Phillips screwdriver
Palm sander

Cut List

Cypress is recommended for this project.

1	Base	3/4" x 8-1/4" x 26"
2	Brush supports	3/4" x 4-1/2" x 9-1/2"
1	Upright	3/4" x 2" x 8-1/4"

Hardware and Supplies

No. 6 x 1-1/4" Deck screws
Stiff 2-1/4" x 7-1/4" brushes (four)

Construction Procedure

1. To make the notch in the 8-1/4" x 26" base, first locate and mark a centerline down its length. Then measure down 3-3/4" along this line, and mark. Make two more marks, 2" to each side of the center at the top edge (see Base Layout).

2. Next, strike a diagonal line from each of the 2" marks to the 3-3/4" mark. With a jigsaw, cut out the notch created by these lines.

3. To round the four corners of the base, measure and mark lines 1" down from each end and 1" in from each side. With a compass, and using the points where these pairs of lines intersect as centers, strike a 1" radius at each corner. Cut along the radius lines

with a jigsaw. Sand all the sides and edges well.

4. To round the two upper corners of each brush support, strike 1" radii at them, just as you did in Step 3. Cut the radii with a jigsaw, and sand the edges smooth.

5. Mount a brush to each of the brush supports, flush with the radiused edge and centered between the ends of the support. Use a No. 6 pilot bit to predrill two holes through the face of each brush; then fasten the brush backs with two No. 6 x 1-1/4" deck screws.

6. Position a brush support on each long edge of the base, 4-3/4" down from its notched end and flush with its bottom surface. Using a No. 6 pilot bit, stopped at 1-1/4", drill two holes through each support and into the edge of the base. Fasten the supports with No. 6 x 1-1/4" deck screws.

7. Secure the two base brushes flush with the ends of the brushes on the supports, using the same method as before.

8. Using the No. 6 pilot bit, stopped at 1-1/4", and two No. 6 x 1-1/4" countersunk screws, mount the upright onto the bottom of the base, 4-3/4" down from the notched end.

9. Sand the project lightly. It requires no finish.

 Tip

If your boots aren't very wide, you may want to cut a narrower base (and shorter upright) so that the brushes on the support pieces will rest closer to each other—and to your boot. Measure the width of your boot, and adjust your cuts accordingly.

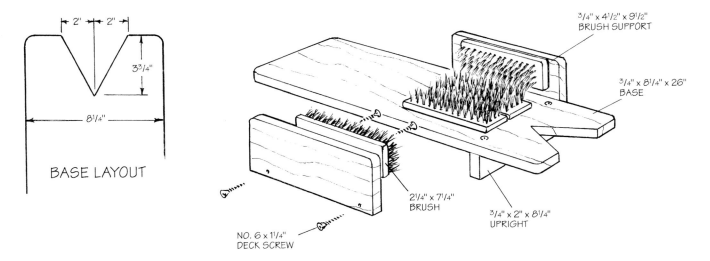

BASE LAYOUT

NO. 6 x 1¼"
DECK SCREW

2¼" x 7¼"
BRUSH

¾" x 2" x 8¼"
UPRIGHT

¾" x 4½" x 9½"
BRUSH SUPPORT

¾" x 8¼" x 26"
BASE

Two-Seater Bench

EVEN THE MOST ENTHUSIASTIC GARDENER NEEDS TO TAKE A BREAK ONCE IN AWHILE, AND WHAT BETTER PLACE TO DO IT THAN OUTDOORS? STURDY IN DESIGN BUT ELEGANT NONETHELESS, THIS GARDEN BENCH WILL PROVIDE AN ATTRACTIVE AND COMFORTABLE RESTING SPOT WHENEVER YOU NEED A MOMENT'S PEACE, AND IT WON'T TAKE MUCH ENERGY TO BUILD, EITHER.

Suggested Tools

Table saw
3/8" Drill
No. 8 Pilot bit and countersink with stop collar
3/32" Drill bit
Router (optional)
3/8" Roundover bit (optional)
Framing square
Tape measure
No. 2 Phillips screwdriver
Rasp
Palm sander

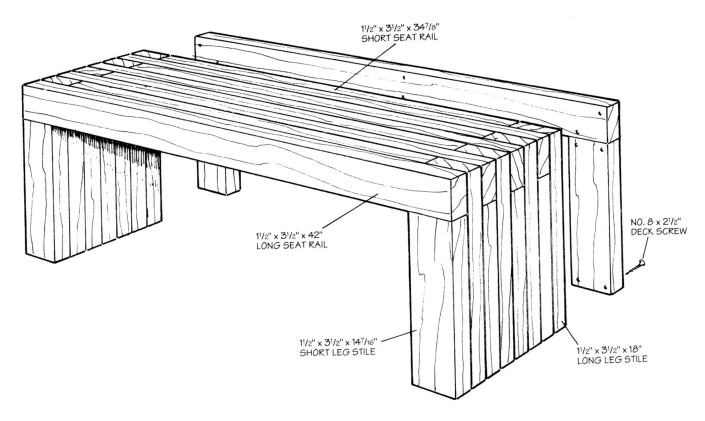

1½" x 3½" x 34⅞" SHORT SEAT RAIL

1½" x 3½" x 42" LONG SEAT RAIL

NO. 8 x 2½" DECK SCREW

1½" x 3½" x 14⁷/₁₆" SHORT LEG STILE

1½" x 3½" x 18" LONG LEG STILE

HOLE PLACEMENT

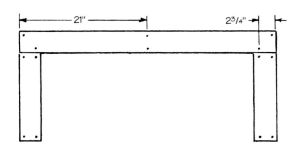

21"   2¾"

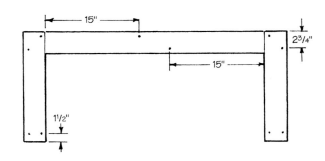

15"   2¾"

15"

1½"

Cut List

Western red cedar is recommended for this project.

5	Long seat rails	1-1/2" x 3-1/2" x 42"
4	Short seat rails	1-1/2" x 3-1/2" x 34-7/8"
8	Long leg stiles	1-1/2" x 3-1/2" x 18"
10	Short leg stiles	1-1/2" x 3-1/2" x 14-7/16"

Hardware and Supplies

Waterproof wood glue
No. 8 x 2-1/2" Deck screws
Exterior clear wood finish (optional)

Construction Procedure

1. Using a 3/32" drill bit, prebore pilot holes (see Hole Placement illustration) through all the rail and stile pieces, except for one 42" rail and two 14-7/16" stiles. Note that most of the holes are 3/4" from an edge or an end, except for the corner-joint bores (at 2-3/4") and the longer leg stile ends (at 1-1/2"). At the center, the holes are 15" from each end on the shorter rails and centered on the longer ones.

2. Start by arranging the three undrilled pieces so that the stiles butt against the lower edge of the rail, and are flush to its ends outside. Use a square to assure that the joints are perpendicular.

3. Place a long (18") stile on each short (14-7/16") stile so that the ends and edges line up. Fasten this pair of long stiles to the rail and stile below, using glue and No. 8 x 2-1/2" deck screws. Countersinking the screws will be easier if you adjust the No. 8 pilot bit to a depth of 1/2" and make the counterbores first, using each predrilled pilot hole as a guide.

4. Apply glue, and then lay a short rail on top of the long rail, between the long stiles that you just fastened, lining up the outside edges. If the fit is tight, use a mallet to tap the piece in place. Counterbore and then fasten as before with No. 8 x 2-1/2" deck screws.

5. Continue alternating sets of rails and stiles until the stack is 13-1/2" wide. If you've drilled the pilot holes according to instructions, no screw will strike the head of a screw in the layer beneath it. To look its best, the bench should begin and end with a long rail on the outside face.

6. To make the seat more comfortable, use a rasp or a 3/8" roundover bit in a router to round the edges of the bench all around. Sand all the surfaces to remove burrs and splinters. Cedar can be left unfinished or coated with an exterior clear wood preservative for a smoother appearance.

FOOTBRIDGE

❧

WE DISCOVERED THIS WELL-DESIGNED FOOT-
BRIDGE ON THE PROPERTY OF A GENTLEMAN IN
HENDERSONVILLE, NORTH CAROLINA, WHO VERY
GENEROUSLY PERMITTED US TO RECREATE ITS
CONSTRUCTION PROCEDURE. THE TECHNIQUES
REQUIRED TO BUILD IT AREN'T COMPLEX,
BUT IF YOU DON'T HAVE ANY EXPERIENCE WITH
CONSTRUCTION PROJECTS, YOU MAY WANT TO ASK
A WOODWORKING FRIEND FOR SOME HELP.

Suggested Tools
Circular saw
Ripsaw
3/8" Drill
No. 10 Pilot bit and countersink with stop collar
3/8" Spade bit
Spade bit extension
Jigsaw
Tape measure
Try square
Framing square
Builder's level
Pipe clamps
No. 2 Phillips screwdriver
Hammer
3/4" Mortise chisel
Chalk line
Adjustable wrench
Post-hole digger
Palm sander

Cut List
Pressure-treated lumber is recommended for this project.

3	Plank supports	3-1/2" x 3-1/2" x 96"
4	End posts	3-1/2" x 3-1/2" x 38"
2	Center posts	3-1/2" x 3-1/2" x 40"
2	Handrails	1-1/2" x 3-1/2" x 96"
13	Planks	1-1/2" x 7-1/4" x 60"

Hardware and Supplies
No. 10 x 2-1/2" Deck screws
No. 10 x 1-1/2" Deck screws
3/4" x 2" Corner brackets (twelve)
3/8" x 6" Carriage bolts and nuts (six)
3/8" Flat washers (six)
4 x 4 Galvanized pier connectors; optional (six)
60 lb. Sacks concrete mix (twelve)
Leather work gloves

Construction Procedure

1. Select a site that's reasonably level and free of large or immovable rocks that will interfere with your placement of the foundation piers. Though the footbridge can be set on bedded cross-timbers, the individual pier method is probably the easiest to accomplish. This design is for an eight-foot bridge; bridges that are longer will require heavier components and may have to be professionally designed.

2. To establish the six points on each side of the bank at which the three plank supports will be level, you can use one of the 8' handrails as a gauge, laying it out in order to mark distances. The centers of the two outer pier connectors at each end of the bridge should be located 54" apart. The distance between pier connector centers across the span of the bridge should be 92". The pier connectors for the center plank support are midway between the outer two connectors on each side of the bridge. Before marking the ground, be sure to check the pitch of the 8' handrail piece.

3. Use a post-hole digger to excavate to a depth of 24" at each of the six points. If your site is not level, you can build 8" x 8" temporary concrete forms from pieces of 2 x 6 and place them over the holes to add extra height to the poured piers. Don't extend the piers higher than 8", though, or you may have to build an extra step at the end of the bridge.

4. Wear leather work gloves. Mix the concrete according to the instructions on the sack, and pour it into the holes until it reaches the edge of the hole or the top of the form. Screed the tops level by scraping them with a piece of 1 x 4. Sink the galvanized pier connectors into the center of each pier, checking to see that their centers are 27" apart in width and 92" across from each other. Allow the concrete to set for a few days.

5. To mortise the ends of the two outer plank supports, first measure 7" from each end of both, and use a square to mark on one side. Locate the centerpoint between the two 7" lines on each support, and make a third mark. Measure 3-1/2" in from the first marks, and make a second line. Then measure 1-3/4" to each side of the center mark, and make two lines. Finally, measure in 1" from the marked edge, and mark a line across the top and bottom of each support, at each place.

6. Set the circular-saw blade to a depth of 1", and cut between the marked lines at the three places on

each girder. Make repeated cuts between the lines to remove the majority of material, and then clean up each mortise with a chisel.

7. To locate the mortises in each post, measure 1" from one end, and use a square to mark a line across the post. Measure over 3-1/2", and make a second line. Measure in 1" from the edge, and mark a line across each of the two adjoining faces. Using the circular saw (and the same cutting method described in Step 6), cut a 1"-deep mortise in each post.

8. Place the unmortised plank support in the center set of pier connectors, and place the other two plank supports to each side, with their mortise cuts facing outward. Clamp one 40" post to the mortise cut in the center of one of the plank supports, and then, using a spade bit, drill a 3/8" hole through the center of the post and the support behind it. Depending on the length of your spade bit, you may have to use an extension to allow the bit to pass completely through the joint. Fasten the post and plank support with a 3/8" x 6" carriage bolt, a flat washer, and a nut. Repeat this procedure on the remaining five posts, keeping in mind that the 38" posts go at the four corners. If a post does not level up properly, try switching two around; you can trim the mortise with a chisel if necessary.

9. Starting at one end of the bridge, place the first 60" plank against the posts, and check with a square to see that the plank is perpendicular to the outer two plank supports. (You can adjust the position of the plank supports slightly by tapping their ends with a hammer.) Once the framing is squared up, fasten the pier connectors to the plank supports with No. 10 x 1-1/2" deck screws.

10. Pull the first plank away from the posts so that approximately 5/8" of the width of the plank hangs over the ends of the plank supports. The plank should overhang the sides evenly. Fasten the plank to the plank supports with three No. 10 x 2-1/2" deck screws at each joint. Predrill the holes with a No. 10 pilot bit, setting the stop collar at 2".

11. The second plank will need to be cut out to fit around the posts. Use a tape measure to determine the inside distance between the posts, and use a square and pencil to mark that distance on plank No. 2, centering it within the length of the board. Then measure the width of the posts, and transfer that width to Plank No. 2, using the square again. When you're planning the layout, remember to take into account a 1/4" spacing between each pair of planks. Use a jigsaw to cut out the notches. Fasten the second plank to the plank supports as before.

12. Continue to fasten the rest of the planks by the same method, leaving a 1/4" gap between each one. Measure and cut notches to fit around the posts where needed. The final plank may have to be ripped lengthwise to allow it to overhang the ends of the plank supports by 5/8".

13. Sight down the ends of the planks from one end of the bridge. If the ends are uneven, snap a chalk line (one that's even with the shortest plank end) between each set of posts. Then trim along the line with a circular saw. (Use a handsaw to cut near the posts).

14. Place a handrail on top of one center post so that its ends overhang the end posts evenly. Use a pair of 2" corner brackets and No. 10 x 1-1/2" deck screws to secure the rail to that post, and then draw the ends of the rail down to the tops of the end posts with the help of a set of pipe clamps. Fasten the ends of the rail with brackets and No. 10 screws as before. Repeat the process on the other hand rail, and remove the clamps once the screws are in place.

15. With a sander, smooth any rough surfaces on the rails and posts. Treated wood requires no finish, but a pigmented deck stain can be used to add color.

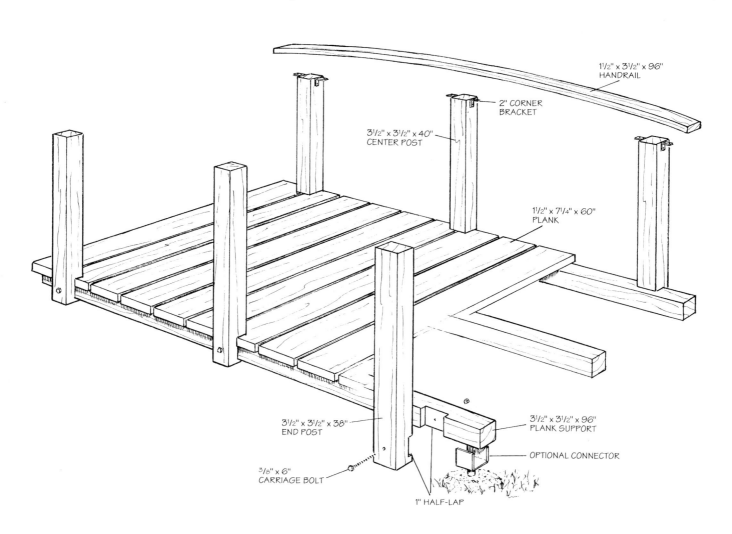

1½" x 3½" x 96"
HANDRAIL

2" CORNER
BRACKET

3½" x 3½" x 40"
CENTER POST

1½" x 7¼" x 60"
PLANK

3½" x 3½" x 38"
END POST

3½" x 3½" x 96"
PLANK SUPPORT

OPTIONAL CONNECTOR

⅜" x 6"
CARRIAGE BOLT

1" HALF-LAP

GAZEBO

WHEN WE DISCOVERED THIS STUNNING GAZEBO, A RECONSTRUCTED HISTORICAL STRUCTURE IN SALUDA, NORTH CAROLINA, WE ASKED CITY OFFICIALS IF WE MIGHT INCLUDE A CONSTRUCTION PROCEDURE FOR IT IN THIS BOOK. FORTUNATELY, SALUDA IS AS GRACIOUS AS ITS ARCHITECTURE IS CHARMING; WE THANK ALL THOSE INVOLVED FOR SHARING THEIR GAZEBO WITH US.

THIS PROJECT IS NOT ONE TO TACKLE IF YOU'RE A BEGINNER. UNLESS YOU'VE HAD A GOOD BIT OF CON-STRUCTION EXPERIENCE, YOU'RE LIKELY TO FIND THE INSTRUCTIONS SOMEWHAT CONFUSING, SO BE SURE TO GET HELP FROM A FRIEND WHO IS FAMILIAR WITH FRAM-ING AND GENERAL CARPENTRY WORK.

Suggested Tools

Table saw
Dado blade
Circular saw
Ripsaw
3/8" Drill
No. 8 Pilot bit and countersink with stop collar
1/2" and 5/8" Spade bits
Tape measure
Framing square
Combination square
Speed square
Carpenter's level
Plumb bob
Line level
C-clamps
Adjustable wrench
Framing hammer
Chalk line
Nylon line
Spade
Extended stepladder

Cut List

Pressure-treated lumber is recommended for this project.

8	Posts	5-1/2" x 5-1/2" x 96"
16	Headers	1-1/2" x 9-1/4" x 78"
8	Rafters	1-1/2" x 5-1/2" x 144"
8	Jack headers	1-1/2" x 5-1/2" x 29-1/2"
16	Cripple rafters	1-1/2" x 5-1/2" x 96"

1	Ridge post	3-1/2" x 3-1/2" x 16"
1	Finial	4-1/2" x 6"
1	Pendant	3-1/2" x 6"
24	Rafter tails	1-1/2" x 3-1/2" x 24"
	Roof decking (T & G)	3/4" x 5-1/2"
	Facia	3/4" x 3-1/2"
104	Header trim (T & G)	3/4" x 5-1/2" x 9-1/4"
	Cap	3/4" x 3-1/2"
	Lower trim	3/4" x 3-1/2"
	Lattice face trim	3/4" x 2-1/2"
8	Lattice supports	1-1/2" x 1-1/2"
	Lattice	1/4" x 8"
7	Upper rails	1-1/2" x 3-1/2"
7	Uprights	1-1/2" x 2-1/4" x 23"
	Lattice	1/4" x 24"
7	Lower rails	1-1/2" x 3-1/2"
7	Seats	1-1/2" x 9-1/4"
14	Seat supports	1-1/2" x 3-1/2"
8	Seat uprights	1-1/2" x 9-1/4" x 15-1/2"
8	Perimeter board	3/4" x 7-1/4" x 79"

Hardware and Supplies

No. 8 x 2-1/2" Deck screws
1/2" x 6" Carriage bolts and nuts (thirty-two)
8d and 16d Galvanized nails
6d Galvanized casing nails
3" Hardened concrete drive screws
3/4" Roofing nails
Roofing felt
Dimensional shingles
Metal drip edge
1/2" x 8" Anchor bolts (eight)
Concrete mix (7-1/2 yds.)
3/4" Gravel
Exterior latex paint

Construction Procedure

1. Begin by selecting a level site that is free of rocks and far enough from trees to allow some freedom from overhead branches and from roots that are close to the soil's surface. Stake out an eight-sided "circle" approximately 16' 4" in diameter (measured from point to point) by establishing eight straight lines between stakes placed 78" apart. Use those as the outside perimeter to excavate a trench footing that is 16" wide and at least 12" deep. (In cold cli-mates, this depth may have to be increased consid-erably; check with local building codes for guide-lines.) Grade the field within the perimeter trench (the area that the gazebo will cover) level at 4" below the existing grade.

2. To assemble an eight-sided perimeter form above ground level for the concrete, use lengths of 2 x 8s placed on both sides of the trench. Nail them at the ends with 2 x 8 scraps, and brace them from the outside with scrap 2 x 4s placed every few feet and staked from 2' away. Using a line level on a nylon string, check the top of the wooden form for level in several directions. Spread gravel on the bottom of the trenches and on the surface of the inside area to a depth of 4". Pour the concrete mix, and screed level with the top of the forms. Before the concrete starts to set up, sink an anchor bolt 6" deep into the pad, 3" inward from each of the eight points of the octagon. Allow the concrete to cure for several days before removing the forms.

3. Drill a 5/8" hole, 2" deep, into the center of each of the eight posts at one end. Then, at the opposite end, locate the center of one face, and on the top of the post, mark angles of 22-1/2° to either side of that point. Measure 2-3/4" back from those lines, and draw two more parallel lines on the top of the post. Now, measure down 9-1/4" from the top surface, and mark a line across the face and two sides with a square. Carry the end of each deeper angled line from the top to its shoulder line on the side, again using the square. Set the depth and angle of your circular saw to make the primary cuts. Then use a handsaw to complete the sides and shoulders.

4. With some helpers, set the posts in place on top of the anchor-bolt stubs at each of the eight points. Check for plumb. At each flat of the octagon, measure for length between the cut notches, and trim the ends of the inner headers to 22-1/2° in opposite directions. Use a temporary nail to hold them in place, flush with the top of the posts. Then measure, trim, and clamp the outer headers to the faces of the inner ones and to the posts. Drill two 1/2" holes, 6" apart, through the center of each header-to-post joint, and fasten with 1/2" x 6" carriage bolts. Drive 16d nails to connect the headers to each other between the bolt sets.

5. Set the table-saw blade at 45°, and trim the long corners of a 16" 4 x 4 to create four 1-1/2"-wide flats. Cut the upper ends of the eight 12' rafters at a 50° angle, and fasten two rafters to opposite flats of this ridge post, 1" below the top end. Temporarily set the rafters in place along opposite posts, and mark the cutlines for the birdsmouths (these are the rafter-joint openings that will rest on the tops and inside faces of the posts; allow about 1-1/2" of contact

length on the inside face if possible). To establish the roof symmetry, locate and mark the exact center of the foundation slab. Then suspend a plumb bob from the middle of the ridge post, and adjust the rafters as needed to make the bob align with that mark. Cut the birdsmouths to suit. Finally, measure, mark, and cut the remaining six long rafters, using the same method and always working with pairs that are opposite one another. Fasten permanently by toe-nailing the joints.

6. At a point 45" from each joint of the ridge post and the lower edge of the rafters, mark a line across the sides of the rafters with a square. Trim eight jack headers to fit these spaces (approximately 29-1/2" in length), and nail them in place.

7. Measure and mark sixteen cripple rafters to fit between the jacks and the doubled headers between the posts below. These are cut square at the upper end but will require birdsmouths where they meet the main headers. Fasten them with 16d nails.

8. Cut the twenty-four rafter tails from 2 x 4s. They are square-cut at the outside end and are trimmed to a 28° angle at the inside. Align each one with the edge at the rafter ends, and fasten with 16d nails.

9. Measure, cut, and fit the roof decking to the rafters, and fasten with 8d nails. The ends of the decking material must be compound (angle and bevel) cut. The project calls for 1 x 6 tongue-and-groove planking because it's visible from below (and thus more attractive), but 3/4" plywood would work if wood waste were not a major concern.

10. Measure, cut, and nail the fascia boards to the ends of the rafters. Remember that the fascia ends have to be beveled to assure a clean fit at the joints. Use 6d nails driven at an angle at the joints and straight-on in between. Measure and install the metal drip edge over the front edges of the decking and fascia.

11. Lay down the roofing felt, and trim it with a utility knife. Be sure to overlap the seams and cap the decking joints for strength. Nail with 3/4" roofing nails so that the points will not penetrate the underside of the decking. Install the shingles in courses, starting at the bottom. Come flush to the drip edge.

12. Fasten the finial and pendant to the ridge post with No. 8 x 2-1/2" deck screws driven at an angle. These can be specially purchased or cut from post stock to a shape of your own design.

13. Measure and cut to length the inner and outer pieces of header trim to face the double headers (these tongue-and-groove pieces go vertically). Fasten with 6d nails. Measure and cut the cap sections at the top of the headers, and fasten them in the same manner, so that they overhang the inner trim by 1-1/4". All pieces end in 22-1/2° angles.

14. Measure the distance between adjoining posts to establish the length of both the lower trim and the lattice face trim. Cut to length with 22-1/2° ends. Fasten the lower trim so that one edge is flush with the joint between the two headers; then fasten the lattice face trim so that its edge is 1/4" from that, to leave a groove for the lattice. Use 6d nails.

15. Use a dado blade in the table saw to cut a 1/2"-deep, 1/4" groove in one face of each 1-1/2" x 1-1/2" lattice support. Measure and cut eight sections each of lattice and support to the lengths necessary to fit

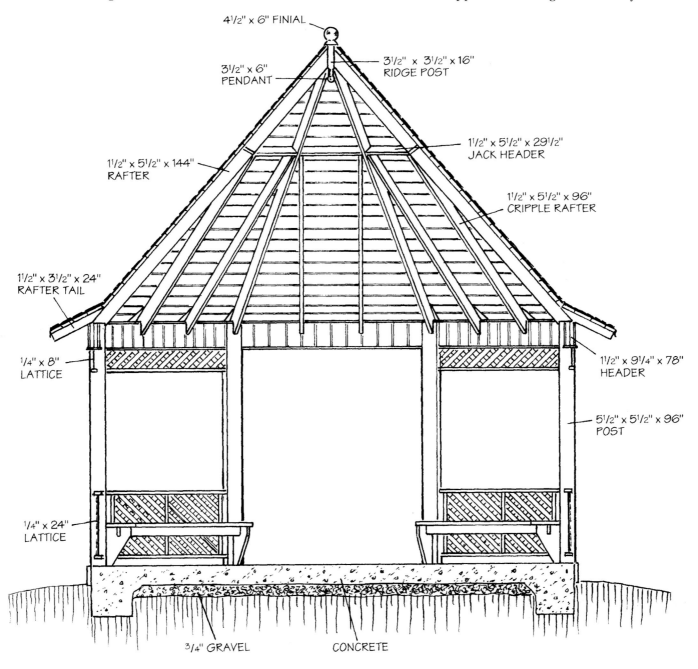

4¹/2" x 6" FINIAL

3¹/2" x 6" PENDANT

3¹/2" x 3¹/2" x 16" RIDGE POST

1¹/2" x 5¹/2" x 144" RAFTER

1¹/2" x 5¹/2" x 29¹/2" JACK HEADER

1¹/2" x 5¹/2" x 96" CRIPPLE RAFTER

1¹/2" x 3¹/2" x 24" RAFTER TAIL

1/4" x 8" LATTICE

1¹/2" x 9¹/4" x 78" HEADER

5¹/2" x 5¹/2" x 96" POST

1/4" x 24" LATTICE

3/4" GRAVEL

CONCRETE

between the faces of the posts. Slip the lattice sections into their grooves, and fasten the supports to the posts with No. 8 x 2-1/2" deck screws. Predrill the holes at an angle, and countersink the heads slightly.

16. Use the dado blade again to cut a 1/2"-deep, 1/4" groove centered in the wide faces of each upper and lower rail. Then cut the same dado grooves into both 2-1/4" faces of each 23" rail upright. Measure the two rails for length between the post sets, and trim the ends accordingly, with 22-1/2° angles. Mark the center of each set of upper and lower rails to position the uprights, and then cut the lattice sections to the appropriate length. Slide the lattice sec-

tions to either side of the center upright, and fasten the upright with 8d nails or No. 8 x 2-1/2" deck screws sunk at an angle. Then fasten the rails to the posts at each side so that the top of the upper rail is 30" above the foundation surface. Use 16d nails or No. 8 x 2-1/2" deck screws set in from the bottom faces.

17. Measure 2" from one edge of each seat upright, and mark at one end. Use the blade of a framing square to draw a line from that point to the opposite corner. Cut along the line on each piece. Fasten the pieces squarely to the center of each post so that the 2" end rests on the foundation slab. Use No. 8 x 2-1/2" deck screws drilled and driven at an angle.

18. Measure and cut the sixteen seat supports so that they fit between each set of uprights. The ends should be beveled at 22-1/2°. Fasten them in pairs, 1" apart, so that the upper edges are flush with the top of the uprights and the front face is 3-1/2" back from the forward edge of those pieces. Countersink No. 8 x 2-1/2" deck screws into the initial ends, and angle-screw the final ends. Measure, cut, and fasten the seats to the top of each assembly. The seat boards are angled at 22-1/2°, and the No. 8 x 2-1/2" screws are fastened from below.

19. Measure, cut, and hammer the perimeter boards in place over the foundation edge. These boards should be beveled at 22-1/2° at both ends. Use hardened concrete drive screws to secure the boards. (As an alternative, you can set masonry anchors into the edges at measured locations, and then fasten the boards with 1/4" lag screws positioned to fit.)

20. Prime all wood surfaces, and paint with a high-gloss exterior latex in the color scheme of your choice. A thin bead of silicone between the finial and the peak shingles will help to prevent wind-blown leaks.

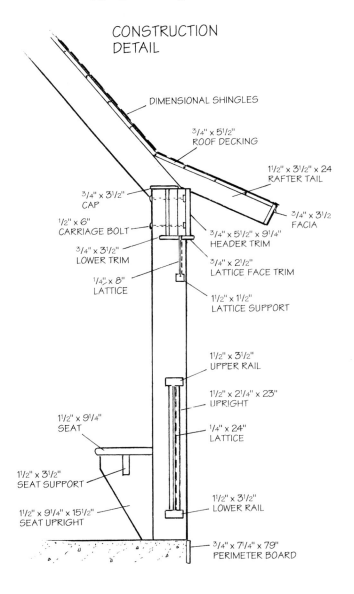

CONSTRUCTION DETAIL

DIMENSIONAL SHINGLES

3/4" x 5 1/2" ROOF DECKING

1 1/2" x 3 1/2" x 24 RAFTER TAIL

3/4" x 3 1/2" CAP

1/2" x 6" CARRIAGE BOLT

3/4" x 3 1/2 FACIA

3/4" x 5 1/2" x 9 1/4" HEADER TRIM

3/4" x 3 1/2" LOWER TRIM

3/4" x 2 1/2" LATTICE FACE TRIM

1/4" x 8" LATTICE

1 1/2" x 1 1/2" LATTICE SUPPORT

1 1/2" x 3 1/2" UPPER RAIL

1 1/2" x 2 1/4" x 23" UPRIGHT

1 1/2" x 9 1/4" SEAT

1/4" x 24" LATTICE

1 1/2" x 3 1/2" SEAT SUPPORT

1 1/2" x 3 1/2" LOWER RAIL

1 1/2" x 9 1/4" x 15 1/2" SEAT UPRIGHT

3/4" x 7 1/4" x 79" PERIMETER BOARD

 Tip

When making a compound cut, one that gives the board an angled face and a beveled edge, always remember to double-check your longest dimensions. The decking boards used on the roof of the Gazebo are positioned with their long faces to the outside and their short edges to the top. Set your table-saw blade to the proper angle (in this case 22-1/2° right), and angle the miter gauge 22-1/2° to the left. Make the cut. Leave the blade where it is, but reset the miter gauge 22-1/2° to the right. Turn the piece end for end, and make the final cut.

ACKNOWLEDGEMENTS

M any thanks to all the people who contributed their projects, their gardens, their advice, and their time. Unless otherwise noted, the generous souls listed below reside or work in Asheville, North Carolina.

Projects

Alan M. Hester, owner of Hester's Lothlorien Barbecue Box, 114-116; Bean Brace, 94-95; Berry Box, 36-37; Boot Bench, 91-93; Cold Frame, 127-129; Compost Bin, 112-113; Drying Rack, 104-106; File Box for Seeds, 122-123; Garden Wagon, 38-40; Handy Box, 47-49; Picnic Table for Two, 55-57; Reversible Bench, 88-90; Seedling Tray, 86-87; Soil Sifter, 83-85; Trash-Bag Holder, 76-77

Mark Strom, also of Hester's Lothlorien Bootjack—and Brush, 130-131; Crossing Signs, 60-62; Cypress Doormat, 58-59; Firewood Brace, 34-35; Flower Truck, 107-109; Garden Gong, 70-72; Hose Guards, 120-121; Hose Wrap, 96-97; Light Box, 80-82; Planter, 73-75; Rail Planter, 98-100; Portable Shade Screens, 124-126; Strawberry Pyramid, 78-79; Sundial, 101-103; Tool-Cleaning Box, 110-111; Tool Shelf, 50-51; Tool Tote, 41-43

Frank Matthews
Bird Feeder, 63-65; Pyramid Plant Stand, 44-46; Squirrel Whirler, 52-54

Kevin McGuire
Potting Bench, 66-69; Two-Seater Bench, 132-133

The City of Saluda, NC
We thank the generous residents of Saluda who gave the author permission to recreate instructions for building the gazebo in that city (138-142).

Charles de Marcay, Hendersonville, NC
We deeply appreciate Mr. de Marcay's permission to recreate his footbridge (134-137) as one of our projects.

The author
Scarecrow Frame, 117-119

Garden Owners

Jean and **Emerson Arnot**

Carol Covington

Miriam and **Harlan Haynes**

Pat and **Roger McGuire**

Anne and **Kevin McGuire**

Chris Rich

Cathy and **Peter Wallenborn**

Illustrations

Don Osby, Page 1 Publications, Horse Shoe, NC

Photography

Evan Bracken, Light Reflections, Hendersonville, NC

Assistance

Edward A. Gibson, Jr., (Secretary\Treasurer) and **Walter Somerville**, both of B.B. Barns, Inc.

Craig Weis, owner of Architectural Woodcraft

METRIC CONVERSION CHARTS

Inches	CM	Inches	CM
1/8	0.3	20	50.8
1/4	0.6	21	53.3
3/8	1.0	22	55.9
1/2	1.3	23	58.4
5/8	1.6	24	61.0
3/4	1.9	25	63.5
7/8	2.2	26	66.0
1	2.5	27	68.6
1-1/4	3.2	28	71.1
1-1/2	3.8	29	73.7
1-3/4	4.4	30	76.2
2	5.1	31	78.7
2-1/2	6.4	32	81.3
3	7.6	33	83.8
3-1/2	8.9	34	86.4
4	10.2	35	88.9
4-1/2	11.4	36	91.4
5	12.7	37	94.0
6	15.2	38	96.5
7	17.8	39	99.1
8	20.3	40	101.6
9	22.9	41	104.1
10	25.4	42	106.7
11	27.9	43	109.2
12	30.5	44	111.8
13	33.0	45	114.3
14	35.6	46	116.8
15	38.1	47	119.4
16	40.6	48	121.9
17	43.2	49	124.5
18	45.7	50	127.0
19	48.3		

Liquids

U.S.	Metric
1 fluid ounce	29.6 ml
1 pint (16 fl. oz.)	473 ml
1 quart (32 fl. oz.)	946 ml
1 gallon (128 fl. oz.)	3.785 l

Weights

1 oz.	28.4 g
1 lb.	453.6 g

SOFTWOOD SIZES

Nominal	Actual
1 x 2	3/4" x 1-1/2"
1 x 3	3/4" x 2-1/2"
1 x 4	3/4" x 3-1/2"
1 x 5	3/4" x 4-1/2"
1 x 6	3/4" x 5-1/2"
1 x 8	3/4" x 7-1/4"
1 x 10	3/4" x 9-1/4"
1 x 12	3/4" x 11-1/4"
2 x 2	1-1/2" x 1-1/2"
2 x 4	1-1/2" x 3-1/2"
2 x 6	1-1/2" x 5-1/2"
2 x 8	1-1/2" x 7-1/4"
2 x 10	1-1/2" x 9-1/4"
2 x 12	1-1/2" x 11-1/4"
4 x 4	3-1/2" x 3-1/2"
4 x 6	3-1/2" x 5-1/2"
6 x 6	5-1/2" x 5-1/2"
8 x 8	7-1/2" x 7-1/2"

INDEX